HOSTILITY WITHIN

A Prophetic Perspective of the Church During the Pandemic

TAVARES D. ROBINSON

Copyright © 2023 Tavares Robinson

www.watchmanpublishing.com

All rights reserved. No part of this publication may be reproduced, stored in a retrieval system or transmitted in any form or by any means—electronic, mechanical, photocopying, recording or otherwise—without the written permission of the author/publisher.

Scripture quotations marked (ESV) are from the ESV® Bible (The Holy Bible, English Standard Version®), copyright © 2001 by Crossway Bibles, a publishing ministry of Good News Publishers. Used by permission. All rights reserved.

Scripture quotations marked (NASB®) are from the New American Standard Bible®, Copyright © 1960, 1971, 1977, 1995 by The Lockman Foundation. Used by permission. All rights reserved. www.lockman.org

Scripture quotations marked (NIV) are taken from the Holy Bible, New International Version®, NIV®. Copyright © 1973, 1978, 1984, 2011 by Biblica, Inc.™ Used by permission of Zondervan. All rights reserved worldwide. www.zondervan.com. The "NIV" and "New International Version" are trademarks registered in the United States Patent and Trademark Office by Biblica, Inc.™

Scripture quotations marked (NKJV) taken from the New King James Version®. Copyright © 1982 by Thomas Nelson. Used by permission. All rights reserved.

Scripture quotations marked (NLT) are taken from the Holy Bible, New Living Translation, copyright ©1996, 2004, 2015 by Tyndale House Foundation. Used by permission of Tyndale House Publishers, Carol Stream, Illinois 60188. All rights reserved.

Cover photography and design by Jesus Cordero
Editing, interior by Rachel L. Hall, Writely Divided Editing & More

Hostility Within: A Prophetic Perspective of the Church During the Pandemic / Tavares D. Robinson —1st edition, 2nd printing.

ISBN: 978-1-7349681-8-7 Paperback
      978-1-7349681-9-4 eBook

Printed in the USA

Contents

Acknowledgments — v

Note to the Reader — vii

Chapter 1	Introduction	1
Chapter 2	Foundations of Prophecy	13
Chapter 3	A Precursor Season: The Signs Emerge	25
Chapter 4	The Foundation of Hostility	55
Chapter 5	The Demise of Ahab	71
Chapter 6	When Loyalty Becomes Lethal	85
Chapter 7	The Lying Spirit	99
Chapter 8	The Downfall of Lies	117
Chapter 9	Wait on the Lord	123
Chapter 10	Discerning Dreams and Truth from Lies	129
Chapter 11	Prophecy Provides Heaven's Perspective	141
Chapter 12	The Barabbas Age	153
Chapter 13	The Countdown to Finality	167
Chapter 14	The Wake of Damage	187
Chapter 15	Spiritual Recovery	201
Chapter 16	The Way Forward	213

About the Author — 231

Acknowledgments

~*~

When the Lord entrusts you with a heavenly mandate, you immediately realize that the responsibility is bigger than one person—it takes a team. I thank the Lord for the team he assembled around me to get this book accomplished. I personally thank Jayda, Jesus, Christina, and Rachel. May the Lord remember your time and labor.

I thank Sound The Trumpet Ministries of Miami for trusting my leadership during and post-pandemic. May the Lord increase our boundaries.

Finally, I thank my Lord and Savior, Jesus Christ, for again trusting me with a message that will transcend time. May your longsuffering toward us yield a harvest of eternal fruit.

~*~

Note to the Reader

Walking the fine line between addressing a problem versus attacking a person is a daunting and often misunderstood task, especially in today's spiritual climate and sensitive church culture, but it's a challenge that must be accepted. I believe it's essential for me to help you clearly understand unpleasant truths and for you, as the reader, to understand my purpose and intentions for writing *Hostility Within*. I warn you, the message in this book is intense. Misinterpreting and misdiagnosing the temperature of this book could lead one to feel provoked or dejected and, consequently, repeat the example of the rich young ruler (Mark 10:17–22). I do not claim to be a licensed clinical expert or the only voice on this matter. Still, my 19 years as a founding pastor of a local church and my travels to various churches throughout the country have given me first-hand knowledge of the recent alarming emotional and spiritual shift among believers.

My aim is not to condemn anyone or to resurrect trauma from the past few years but to indict so that through true repentance, we can all be acquitted. My tone may sometimes seem severe and challenging, but joy and hope are promised. In the end, you'll understand that only God can take a tragic and tender situation and make it work out for your good.

Finally, as you read, you will notice particular biblical truths repeated. I included this repetition on purpose to emphasize important subjects and as a teaching tool to help you fully comprehend. We learn by repetition. Therefore, as a leader who is charged with overseeing God's flock, I believe I should teach things that have to be retaught. However, I hope I never teach things that have to be unlearned. Scriptural truths demand repetition, especially since we live in a time when many things are being redefined and repackaged. Even Christ repeated various themes over and over in his teachings. He desired to help those who had "an ear to hear" learn and remember what he said (John 16:4). Being an overcomer in these Last Days will require us to become one with the word of God by continually remembering what the word says.

May the words of King David be a plumb line in the challenging days to come. In reference to those who are in right standing with God: "They have made God's law their own, so they will never slip from his path" (Ps. 37:31 NLT).

~Tavares D. Robinson

HOSTILITY
WITHIN

Chapter 1

Introduction

2020: THE YEAR WILL FOREVER BE ETCHED IN OUR MINDS. From young children to the elderly, from the United States to Australia, no one escaped the adversity that earmarked the decade's opening. The year was marked by significant loss—many lost their sense of financial security, physical health, and spiritual vitality. Countless people lost their lives. The extreme anxiety and pain we experienced were worsened by ever-increasing incidents of hypocrisy, impulsivity, vitriol, and lies, culminating in deep-seated divisiveness—even among previously united groups. In the US, disturbing social events were punctuated by overwhelming turbulence that stirred up an upheaval of rage and the expression of unbridled passions. Combined with the deadly, out-of-control pandemic, these emotions resulted in conflict, confusion, and chaos.

At the time of this writing, the COVID-19 pandemic has claimed over 900 thousand deaths in the US alone and will perhaps go down as the most dangerous viral crisis in this country's history. It has not just negatively impacted society at large, but it has also uncovered ungodly, undesirable fruit within the church. The reaction of the redeemed to various aspects of the pandemic—whether the shut-down mandates, masking requirements, or vaccines—has been far from admirable. The called-out ones—those supposed to be salt and light—have behaved in ways hard to distinguish from the ways of the world. Under the guise of "defending my truth," Christians have displayed deep-seated hatred, betrayed others, and committed acts of revenge that operate in tandem with secular political activism, selfish nationalism, and whatever other latest-trending catchphrases that should not be named among Christ's followers. And sadly, such heartbreaking things have not only created an unhealthy tribalism among the Tribe (the body of Christ), but they have disrupted the foundation of faith, trust, and confidence of many of those who love Christ and the community of believers. Many have grown disillusioned by and uninterested in the church because it has become less Christ-like and more political. Some churches have become less bible-centered and more therapy-driven. Unfortunately, for some of us, our views of God and the church have been tarnished, and our hearts have been bruised by angry and vengeful Christians who allowed misguided opinions, personal preferences and biases to unhinge previously godly relationships.

How did we get here? Did 2020, one year alone, produce this much turmoil, division, dismantling, deception, and deconstruction?

***

We live in a time when words are defined and redefined to meet individuals' personal preferences, so I want to explain what I mean by the term *deconstruction*. I will use the term often throughout this book, and I realize that others define it differently than I do. Some use *deconstruction* to describe the act of reevaluating beliefs to reject falsehoods and reaffirm a foundation of truth. However, that is not how I use the word. I use it to describe the act of abandoning scripture-focused Christianity for some subtly (or not so subtly) alternative version of Christianity or for leaving Christianity as a whole. Many begin deconstructing their faith in this way because they have been persuaded by belief systems that do not originate from the Holy Spirit. The Holy Spirit spoke with urgency and precise clarity through the apostle Paul to warn us against this type of deconstruction: "But the Spirit explicitly says that in later times some will fall away from the faith, paying attention to deceitful spirits and doctrines of demons, by means of the hypocrisy of liars seared in their own conscience as with a branding iron" (1 Tim. 4:1–2 NASB).

When Paul writes, "the Spirit explicitly says," he is not making a false claim. He has become an oracle through which the Spirit communicates to the church. What the Spirit says to Paul is clear, open, and direct. There should be no misunderstanding about what the Spirit is communicating. He is repeating what has been spoken before.

When we read, "in later times some will fall away from the faith," Paul indicates a period following the time he was writing. Then, people will ignore the church, defect from the truth, and take the wrong path. They may profess Christianity, but they will deny essential doctrine. In other words, they will apostatize or deliberately abandon the truth they once counted dear for something contrary to the truth. What will they abandon? The faith. Paul is not referring to Christian professions of faith. He is talking about Christian doctrine, the body of teachings that has not changed throughout history. It is the same faith Jude mentions in his epistle: "Dear friends, although I was very eager to write to you about the salvation we share, I felt compelled to write and urge you to contend for the faith that was once for all entrusted to God's holy people" (Jude 3 NIV).

The idea of deceitful or seducing spirits comes from the Greek word *planos*, from which we get the word *planet*. It means to wander or rove.

There are evil, supernatural spirits who aim to lead people astray by causing them to wander from the truth (Gal. 5:7–10). These misleading and deceiving spirits constantly lead in a way that has no fixed destination.

So, when Paul mentions the "doctrine of demons" (1 Tim. 4:1), the reference is not to demonology, which is teaching on demons. Instead, it relates to teachings inspired, suggested, and given by demons—teachings formulated by Satan, who uses people as the mouthpieces of error (2 Pet. 2:1–3). The teaching comes "by means of the hypocrisy of liars," according to Paul (1 Tim. 4:2). These liars appear authentic but are pretenders and imposters, and they speak false truths. Such deceitful teachers are addicted to the lies they tell (Matt. 23:25–28).

So, in essence, Paul warned about a future when people would attach, join, or come into agreement with dangerous teachings that would alter their belief systems. Unfortunately, we are living in those times.

***

I've seen the type of deconstructing I've defined here even among my fellow Black American believers. Emotions can run high when a mixture of secular, social, and political issues intertwine with theological practices and beliefs. When racial tensions reached a climax during the beginning of the pandemic, cultural hostility arose, even within the Black community. For example, regarding the wrongful death of George Floyd, many took the approach, "You either with us or against us." In the Black church in particular, if your view was not in harmony with theirs, you were considered *not black enough*.

Now, place this modern tragedy in the context of spiritual faith: Jesus was unjustly murdered by oppressors, and the 400 years of Hebrew slavery in the Bible is mirrored in the 400 years of Black slavery in America. Backlash and division, and contrasting opinions of how we should interpret biblical precedent, historical events, and modern incidents, resulted in many Blacks walking away from the church, and in particular from what some define as White American Christianity. While they walked away from both Black and White churches, more left majority White churches. Because 2020 was an election year, political party allegiance also played a role.¹ Because more Blacks follow White pastors than Whites follow Black pastors, the visual was used to paint the picture of oppression. So, some Blacks rejected the church because they came to view it as an oppressive system, unrepresentative of their culture or history. However, in doing so, they opened themselves to belief systems focused on color-centered rather than Christ-centered theology.

What did this reveal? It revealed that it didn't matter how much people proclaimed the name of Jesus and his church before 2020 because, in that one year, the faith of many collapsed like a deck of cards.² I asked the question before: did one year cause all this? The answer is no. The hostility within the church and within our own hearts has been lurking under the radar for years. Then, the unstable climate of 2020 produced an atmosphere primed for a stormy outburst. We ended up in a tsunami. A tsunami is a catastrophic ocean wave, a byproduct of a disturbance that has erupted beneath the water's surface. And even though a tsunami itself can be deadly, it's a manifestation of a deeper problem.

***

I wrote *Hostility Within* with three distinct purposes in mind:

---

[1] White evangelical church members have traditionally aligned with the GOP. According to Pew research, 56% of members of White Evangelical Protestant groups report as Republican/lean Republican, compared with 10% of members of historically Black Protestant groups. https://www.pewresearch.org/religion/religious-landscape-study/party-affiliation#party-affiliation.

[2] Institute of Family Studies research suggests that 20 million people stopped attending church due to the pandemic, or a six percent attendance decline from 2019 to 2021, and 57 percent in the US report never or rarely attend church. See Nathan Vanderklippe's "COVID-19 has taken a toll on churchgoing in America as country shifts its views on religion," *The Globe and Mail*, 1/23/2022. https://www.theglobeandmail.com/world/article-covid-19-has-taken-a-toll-on-churchgoing-in-america-as-country-shifts/.

- **First, to help the body of Christ navigate around spiritual quicksand and destructive land mines, for they are only the beginning.** Divisiveness, hatred, harassment, betrayal, resentment and distrust will increase in the future; therefore, we need to learn to discern the way and how to walk circumspectly through difficult times with integrity, faith, and hope.

- **Second, to pull up those who have become victims of the adversity and to rescue those who have been kidnapped by the deep hurt, bitterness and anger that has been cultivated in their hearts.** Many have turned their backs on Christ and his church. They harbor hostility concerning the things of God, and that hostility has reshaped their perspective. Many who used to cherish and look forward to attending weekly services are starting to believe that being a part of a local fellowship is no longer necessary. Hearts once full of passion and devotion have turned cold and callous.

- **Third, to reach wounded and overwhelmed pastors.** Many pastors have experienced burnout from a conflagration of spiritual and political animosity.[3] Many no longer lead with joy but feel obligated to obey the calling. Some have reached a breaking point and are searching for ways to remove themselves from pastoral responsibilities. Others have resigned.[4]

---

[3] For details, see Tish Harrison Warren's "Why Pastors Are Burning Out," *The New York Times*, Aug. 28, 2022.
[4] Barna research shows 38% of pastors considered quitting in 2021. Cited in Vanderklippe, above.

We are called *sheep* by divine design (Ps. 100:3; Isa. 53:6). Why? From a natural perspective, sheep flock together. They are *flockers*, if I may, not *deserters*. Sheep have an intensely social disposition that allows them to bond closely with other sheep, especially during times of danger. This flock mentality protects individual sheep from harmful predators. Sheep are prey; therefore, their help must come from outside themselves. Sheep are created to be led, not to lead. While democracy has its rightful place as a secular form of government, some of its principles of self-rule and the consequent love of self create the delusion that even as the sheep of God's pasture, we should self-govern. That's not a reality in the animal kingdom, but despite our God-given identification as sheep, we have become convinced of our presumed right to self-govern within the church. However, contrary to this growing opinion, we cannot biblically love, serve, and honor Christ if we do not let him lead as our shepherd, and we additionally hate and belittle his bride, the church.

Within the church, we have become so broken and frustrated that some might find it offensive that I intend to reach out to wounded pastors. Let me reassure you: I'm well aware of clergy members' scandalous behavior, abuse, and mishandling of God's sheep in the church. In 2010, I wrote *Shepherds, Hirelings and Dictators: How to Recognize the Difference* and in 2020 released a revised tenth-anniversary edition on how to identify and escape spiritual neglect. I have no desire to aid and abet wolves in shepherd's clothing, enemies of the cross. However, despite unbiblical things happening among leadership, God has a remnant of pastors who love Christ and his church more than anything and are willing to put everything on the line to glorify and honor Christ. These are the pastors we should be praying for, supporting and cheering on (Heb. 13:17). We desperately need them in clerical uniforms and not in civilian clothing (2 Tim. 2:1–4).

If, over the last few years, you have found yourself navigating quicksand, facing adversity, or been deeply wounded, know that God is merciful and longsuffering, not willing that anyone be lost. Providentially, this book may be God's way for you to redirect the trajectory of your thinking and, subsequently, your actions.

***

During the pandemic, contention and confusion reached a point of extreme frustration for many inside the church. Why was this happening? Satan works hard to keep his agenda hidden and covert because you cannot resist and overcome that which you can't see. But I've learned that half the battle is won when you understand what's happening. So, I started praying and asking God to show me how, as a pastor, I should lead those under my care. One day while reading through the book of Second Chronicles, I reached a familiar story. I had read it many times before, but the plot leaped off the pages this time. Things I never noticed before were now clear. At that moment, I realized God was giving me my answer. He was not only granting me clarity to share with my local congregation. No: I realized this message was for the church at large.

Second Chronicles 18 reveals a prophetic picture of what I believe the body of Christ looks like pre- and post-pandemic, from heaven's perspective. Eight characters in this scene reflect personality traits currently operating in the body of Christ: Ahab, Jehoshaphat, the false prophets, Micaiah, the people, Zedekiah, the lying spirit, and God. In later chapters, we'll explore these together as they offer a panoramic view of how God sees the body of Christ. We can avoid God's disapproval by learning how to identify undesirable character traits in others in order to recognize how those traits can linger unnoticed within our own hearts. (Having the mindset that everybody you encounter is toxic, unloving and narcissistic, but you are good, can undeniably be a sign of spiritual delusion.)

This might not be the most palatable chapter in the Bible, but when it comes to medicine, sweet and pleasant things are not true remedies for a disrupted digestive system. We tend to search for cures that make us happy and cheerful during times of pain and turmoil. But those things only work as temporary placebos. The deliverance, healing, and recovery that comes when we follow Christ may require us to digest what's bitter and unpleasant but necessary.

Even though the chapter is intense, it is measured in the end by God's mercy. Undesirable circumstances have a way of producing undeniable victories if we follow the Lord's leading. Therefore, we need to look at our life and circumstances through a new lens to overcome the hostility within.

***

Learning how to evaluate and assess the times is a primary priority. Jesus chided the spiritual leaders of Israel who knew how to discern the weather but were blind to the times (Matt. 16:1–3). They were not spiritually sensitive enough to recognize and adjust to the appearance of Christ. Likewise, if we are improperly prepared to discern the time we live in and the time to come, turmoil may mark our spiritual journey, even to the point of jeopardizing our eternal destination.

I aim to show you from a new perspective what we have faced during the pandemic and what we can learn from it. With hindsight as a teaching tool, we can uncover the past to improve our current insights and shape our spiritual foresight. Christ is returning for a church without spot or wrinkle. It will be a rigorous process to get to that finished state, for the spots must go through a scrupulous purification process, and every wrinkle must have scorching heat applied to become smooth.

I believe God allowed the ills of the pandemic to force believers to rethink our temporary stay in this world (Heb. 11:13–16) and to challenge us to revisit the sometimes agonizing but blissful journey of biblical discipleship. True discipleship is not seeker-friendly; it's a process of discomfort and loss (Luke 9:56–62). The first lesson in biblical discipleship is never about gaining; it's about losing—losing your life, desires, selfish ambitions, dreams, and even your reputation (Mark 8:34–35). Sadly, this view of discipleship has been neglected and even discarded in this age of consumerism Christianity.

The church is a battleship and is never supposed to be at ease in a land of war (Eph. 6:12–18). I'm reminded of this truth: without the persecution of Saul of Tarsus, who eventually became the apostle Paul (Acts 9:1–19), the church would have remained in its comfort zone in Jerusalem (Acts 8:1–8). But Christ commanded the disciples to go to Jerusalem, Judea, Samaria, and the other parts of the world (Acts 1:8). In his sovereignty, God allowed an uncomfortable situation to shake the early church out of its complacency, and he is still doing that today.

***

Sometimes when we are in pain, a different type of pain provides the cure. For example, an excruciatingly painful injury may require grueling surgery as the only hope for healing. Surgery may repair the damage, but it likely won't immediately eliminate the pain. It's now a different pain; it's the pain of recovery. And when it's time for rehabilitation, the pain can become so intense and unbearable that we wonder if we can finish. But afterward, we learn we can press through. Perhaps we'll even come to cherish the pain we endured because vitality and strength are the final outcomes.

Suppose someone is hospitalized for methicillin-resistant *Staphylococcus aureus* (MRSA), and their doctor only prescribes Tylenol. In that case, the physician could be sued for medical malpractice if the person suffers harm from the disease. The person didn't need Tylenol. They needed a more potent, targeted medicine, like Vancomycin. Some medicines have unpleasant side effects we'd rather not endure, but frequently, when the benefits outweigh the side effects, it's worth the risk of taking the medicine. Our spiritual body is in such a crisis that we need powerful but potentially pain-inducing treatment to rectify the dilemma we're in. I believe that the message in this book is part of the radical remedy we need.

We live in a fragile, fractured church environment where hard words are construed as unloving and not graceful. The command to "speak the truth in love" has been supplanted with the belief that we should not say anything that might be considered offensive. We have become so easily triggered that we are conditioned to accept any message that seems pleasant. When the serpent deceived Eve in the Garden of Eden, it was not how he said what he said that moved her into disobedience, but it was what he said (Gen. 3:4–5). We need to place as much importance on what is said instead of basing our decision to receive a message on how it's said.

The message in this book is a word of exhortation. It's an urgent call. Time has been lost, and we don't have a lot of room to right this ship. The word *exhortation* doesn't mean to just encourage someone. It also means to press, apply force to, and press the mind or will by arguments and persuasion (Heb. 13:22). As a body of believers, we are in a critical time, and it's imperative that we make difficult but right decisions. Some of the things we experienced in 2020 will be repackaged in 2024 on a more intense scale. And as we are already in a fragmented state, what's coming has the potential to reshape the church in an undesirable way for years to come. The church needs to be examined, diagnosed and freshly equipped to face a new time of diabolical division, fascism, racial hate, lies, deception, and broken relationships. It is God's will that the church is strengthened to stand in the midst of these flash floods of falsehoods, these evil times (Eph. 6:13). We cannot resist what we cannot discern, and we cannot accurately discern what we must resist unless our minds have been recalibrated to the ways of God. I pray that this book will reshape your discernment in these unsettling times so you may be victorious over the strategic wiles of your adversary.

Please understand it's not all gloom and doom for the church, for we know Jesus' words still stand true. He will build his church, and the enemy will not have victory. But we have to build in such a way that Satan doesn't take more from the church than granted, for it is not Christ's will that we are ignorant of our adversary's devices (2 Cor. 2:11). We have to become better stewards of our brothers' and sisters' needs, especially in the moments of battle. Moreover, we can't endure what we can't overcome, and we can't overcome unless we see things from God's point of view. If God's truth has not become our template, then a lie will seek to become our teacher.

Chapter 2

Foundations of Prophecy

More than ever, the church needs the voice of a prophet. We are desperate for those who stand in the functioning gift of a prophet (Eph. 4:11) and not just those who may have the gift of prophecy (1 Cor. 12:10). Those with the gift of a prophet have been deeply tested and approved by God: they have a divine unction to function. They are sent by God to recover difficult and challenging parts of the faith that have been replaced by relativism and deconstructionism. These prophets understand their time and what God is communicating to the people of that time. Prophets have five points to their purpose:

1. to make God's agenda known to his people;
2. to make individuals aware of their heart's perspective;
3. to reorient God's people to his timing;
4. to spiritually recover what has been forsaken or neglected; and
5. to turn people back to God's heart.

The Voice of a Prophet

We don't call for lawyers, loan officers, psychologists, or philosophers in medical emergencies. Instead, we call for Emergency Medical Technicians (EMTs). EMTs are trained and certified to diagnose and provide immediate treatment for health conditions under the pressure of life or death. Prophets are God's agents in times of spiritual crisis. A prophet's appearance indicates God is coming to make a demand and a deal. A prophet stands between the mercy and the judgment of God. Think of Jonah. He was reluctant to obey God's command to preach judgment to his enemies because he knew there was a chance for them to change and for God to forgive them for their abhorrent sins (Jon. 4:1–2). But, as he obeyed God's instructions, Jonah was placed between mercy and judgment (Jon. 3:1–10).

In many cases, mercy is forfeited without the coming of prophets. We desperately need prophets, but as in previous generations, we do not welcome them (Acts 7:52). Prophets are not well received because they usually bring a hard word to callous hearts (Jer. 7:25–27). They have to say what is difficult for people to spiritually digest and do so in a climate where people have an appetite for sweet nothings from popular preachers who tell them what they want to hear.

When God's people fail to embrace and humbly submit to the truthfulness of his word and instead give themselves to faddish and duplicitous rhetoric, the culture around them starts to decay. When our pulpits no longer echo God's authentic, prophetic word but become springboards for political pandering and clichés, Satan will choose diabolical polarization as his tool. When the voice of God is silenced during times of panic, upheaval, confusion, and skepticism, Satan looks to fill the void with voices that parade conspiracies, unjust hatred, and religious lies. In the final days of ancient Judah before the Babylonian captivity—which I firmly believe parallels the current time in the us—the people grew weary of the prophetic voice of Jeremiah, which created a platform and an audience for the pseudo-prophet Hananiah (Jer. 28:1–17).

When false narratives are constantly repeated, that which is true will begin to sound unpleasant, as if it were lacking empathy, irrelevant, and even untrue. The further God's people drift from the truth, the more they disdain those who remind them of that truth. You see, during times of spiritual defection and deception when the demand for self-governing is exalted (Judges 17:6), and rebellion is glorified, the last voice welcomed is the voice of a prophet. Why? Because a true prophet of the Lord is not sent by God to confirm and cheer people's desires and expectations or the idolatry of humanism (Jer. 27:14–17). The prophet's voice will either bring peace to conflicted souls as they proclaim repentance or stir up rage, vengeance, and disdain in the hearts of those who pursue idols. Humanism places our needs, desires, comforts, and wills at the center of God's plan, and the prophet is an enemy to anything that seeks to compete, replace, and remove God from his rightful place.

Biblically, whenever God's people departed from his original divine intentions, prophets were sent out to win them back from apostasy (Jer. 7:1–14). Thus, every biblical prophet understood God's history concerning his people. Their assignment was to measure the current generation against the past. God's future is in his history. God declares the end from the beginning, not the end (Isa. 46:10). The key to moving in the Spirit is not moving toward new things that did not originate with God. Instead, it's rediscovering the things of old—spiritual truths handed down for generations—that have been forsaken, neglected, and discarded along the way (2 Kings 22:8–20). British preacher T. Austin Sparks once said, "A prophet's calling is only necessary when things have departed from God's original agenda."[1] Therefore, the appearance of true prophets indicates God's people have moved far away from his

---

[1] T. Austin Sparks, *Prophetic Ministry: A Classic Study on the Nature of a Prophet* (Shippensburg: Destiny Image Publishers, 2000). See Chapter 1, "What Prophetic Ministry Is."

intention. In the Old and New Testaments, prophets were not normally sent to the world: in fact, only Jonah was sent to unbelievers (Jon. 1:2). Instead, prophets were sent to those married to God but living in spiritual adultery (Jer. 3:14, Ezek. 3:4–6).

From the voice of Noah in Genesis to the warnings of Jesus in Revelation, God has always desired to turn the hearts of his people back to him through the ministry of the prophets. "The LORD, the God of their ancestors, sent word to them through his messengers again and again, because he had pity on his people and on his dwelling place" (2 Chron. 36:15 NIV). God trusted prophets' voices in times of spiritual emergency. For King Saul, there was a Samuel (1 Sam. 15:1–35); for King Jeroboam, there was the young prophet and Ahijah (1 Kings 13:1–13; 14:1–18); for King Ahab, there was an Elijah and a Micaiah (1 Kings 18:1–45; 22:8); for King Jehoiakim, there was a Jeremiah (Jer. 26:1–24); and for the nation of Israel, there was a John the Baptist (Luke 3:1–20).

The Role of a Prophet

God does not send prophets for us to celebrate and enshrine them. He sends them because he has a disagreement with his people. Prophets are not sent to be relevant and trendy in response to a culture driven by its latest obsessions and popular buzzwords. They are sent to proclaim a message that opposes the norm to turn God's people's hearts back to him (Luke 1:16). No true prophets have been popular in their day because their ministries are a calling of reaction and not of proaction (Ezek. 2:3–8). They are sent by God to those who have deviated from his original path. Most prophets call for repentance: they want to bring God's people back to his original plan so they can once again discern his course (Jer. 6:16).

Biblical prophets were like God's alarm clocks—irritating and disturbing but necessary to awaken a people entranced by deception and worldliness. People respond to prophets in two ways: they can wake up or reject the message. Prophets were heaven-appointed litigators sent to announce *guilty* charges upon God's people who had transgressed and slid from absolutes yet believed they were innocent. Mark this down: Biblical prophets were covenant prosecutors, not government-supporting spokespersons. The only prophets who supported and defended human governments in the Bible were false prophets: Balaam, Ahab's prophets, Hananiah, and the False Prophet, who will affirm the Antichrist in the coming days. So, we should beware of those dressed in prophetic clothing who inwardly are hired, political lobbyists.

Prophets are not people pleasers. They are driven by a desire to be found faithful to the Lord. They cannot be bribed by the world, for they are employees on God's payroll. There is a common thread among prophets sent by God in the Bible: all are out of sync with their generation. Although they seem out of touch with the times, they are in harmony with heaven (1 Kings 22:12–14). Prophets don't desire to be trendy; their passion is to be found trustworthy. Since they deliver messages specific to God's people, what they say is irrelevant to the broader culture. Thus, they are considered outdated, unloving, and too critical by the masses because their message is not fashioned by time but by eternity. They are labeled *traitors* by the undiscerning but are found loyal by God. Time—not majority opinion—validates their assignment's accuracy and truthfulness. Unlike Samson, true prophets will never rest their heads in the lap of cultural relevancy (Judges 16:19), but like John the Baptizer, they are willing to risk their heads for being culturally indifferent (Matt. 14:1–12). They are an enigma to their generation but find understanding and favor with those born out of due time. Even the prophet Christ said, "No prophet is accepted in his own country" (Luke 4:24 NKJV).

Think of the prophet Samuel in the days when Israel wanted a king to be like the rest of the nations (1 Sam. 1:1–22). Israel mourned when

Samuel died but disregarded his words while he was alive (1 Sam. 28:3). Prophets are usually more appreciated and respected after they are gone. However, their contemporaries regard them as contentious, combative, and narrow-minded because their appearance means it is time to make a decision. And there are only two choices: go God's way or suffer the consequences for rejecting it. So, prophets are abhorred, rejected, and treated with contempt. Some are even killed because they are viewed as a hindrance—a thorn in the side of people who pursue their own desires while falsely claiming God's blessing (Matt. 23:34–35).

From the Hebrew prophets through to Christ, every prophet who had a public ministry was incorrectly diagnosed because the people married the message they proclaimed to the messenger's heart. People will frequently misdiagnose the heart of others as an excuse for rejecting the message. Biblical prophets physically experienced the conflict between God and his people as the people carried out on the prophets what they really wanted to dish out on God (Acts 7:51–59).

Prophets have never been politically correct or fascinated by surfing with the times. Their message goes against the current flow because it is fashioned out of a counter-cultural perspective of eternity. Revivalist Vance Havner said, "God's man needs to adjust only to God's Word and God's will. It is not the business of the prophet to harmonize with the times."[2] Ministries that don't challenge the current times are in danger of being self-ordained and illegitimate. In the words of author Malcolm Muggeridge, "Never forget that only dead fish swim with the stream."[3] None of God's work in the scriptures flowed from the current streams of that day. A. W. Tozer said, "I'd rather stand with God and have the world my enemy, than to go along with the crowd to destruction."[4]

---

[2] Vance Havner, *The Best of Vance Havner*. Grand Rapids, MI: Baker Publishing Group, 1989.
[3] Gregory Wolfe, *Malcom Muggeridge: A Biography*. Wilmington, DE: Intercollegiate Studies Institute, 2003.
[4] A. W. Tozer, "In Everything by Prayer," Audio Sermon.

What Prophecy Is and Is Not

While on this note, based on what we see frequently paraded among us today, it's important to establish another truth: God has never raised up prophets to be driven by money or to become hired guns to raise large offerings. Prophets driven by profit are false prophets. In fact, the constant proclaiming of some transfer of wealth and a telethon-style of raising money that's usually attached to a promise if you give the required amount are two clear signs that a prophet is untrue. So beware: The gifts of the Spirit and money do not mix. Ask Simon (Acts 8:9–24)! I am convinced that if Simon were alive today, a lot of leaders would take his "seed faith" money, anoint him, and give him an eldership position.

If you are in a church service and begin to see spiritual gifts operating with the goal of raising money, run. It does not matter how authentic the gifts may appear: if they are profit-driven, they do not indicate an authorized move of the Spirit of the Lord. If we overlook the flaws, choose to believe such individuals are speaking on behalf of Christ, and do not silence them, we are partially responsible for keeping deranged and delusional spokespersons in operation (2 John 2:9–11).

What is in our hearts that we fall for and even covet such diabolical rubbish? In some ways, it's like an addiction we must keep feeding. How many times do we have to be promised that if we sow a seed, we will see millions of dollars before the year is out? How many more messages do you need to hear about coming out of debt if you give a particular amount of money? How many times are you going to believe in your spiritual leader about "investing" in the next newest thing that's really a pyramid scheme? Truth be told, the only people who will receive a "return" will be your leader and any wolf they invite in to fleece the wool of the flock. How many times will you believe that if you sow a seed, God is going to save your marriage or your loved ones? Interestingly, the people who tell you to sow a seed for your marriage often end up divorced.

> *Prophets driven by profit are false prophets.*

I must note that those who teach and prophesy a lie about a transfer of the world's wealth never receive their wealth from the world. They receive it from naïve, misled, and covetous people in the church. Should we, as believers, honor the Lord in our giving and have a willing heart to share our wealth with others? Absolutely. In 2 Corinthians 8 and 9, the scriptures compel us to give sacrificially, so please don't misconstrue what I'm saying. I have been preaching and pastoring long enough to know that people tend to misinterpret what you say when the message contradicts their expectations or beliefs. When a message runs counter to peoples' desires, they have the potential to hear things you are not saying. I'm referencing modern-day Balaams, who were once restricted to being on television and in the pulpit, but now float freely on social media outlets while highlighting their Cash App, PayPal, and Zelle accounts you can give to. They are false spokespersons sent by Satan. They announce bogus promises in the name of God, place stumbling blocks in the lives of those immature in their faith, and tarnish God's name among the unbelieving (2 Pet. 2:1–3; Jude 9–11; Rev. 2:14). Be wary of those well-known for their blue check status, but not for prophetic and biblical accuracy.

Prophets were sent by the Lord as his last sign of mercy to a people who were no longer moving forward but had begun to walk backward (Jer. 7:23–27). Their willingness to please God and do his will compelled them to parachute down into an avalanche of unbiblical syncretism, apostasy, spiritual stubbornness, deceit, and insidious lies, just to save the souls of those who assumed they were in right standing with the Lord. They were sent to people who preferred falsehoods over what was true and preferred the temporal over that which is eternal. Their messages were undesirable, unpleasant and challenging to swallow (Amos 7:10–13). Nevertheless, their messages served as a call to action—an ultimatum, if you will—giving such charge in times when people's desires became their gods. As a result, speaking up placed these prophets on the most wanted list because a biblical ultimatum will never sit well with an opinionated culture (Jer. 26:7–11).

In the book of Revelation, Jesus gave five out of seven churches such charges. He gave them a this-or-that choice. Such prophetic declarations are often met with hostility and vicious rhetoric from the recipients. For example, during the days of the prophet Isaiah, when lying was exalted above the truth, people demanded the prophets stop prophesying that which did not support or encourage their personal agendas. Instead, they expected to hear pleasant and comforting words (Isa. 30:8–11). In Jeremiah's case, when Israel was experiencing external disturbances that looked unfair, unfavorable, and unjust, his words did not foster the type of edification, positive motivation, personal confirmation and nationalism the people were looking for. So, he was treated as a false, disconnected enemy, while the unauthorized and unapproved voice was validated, esteemed, and treated as a friend (Jer. 20:1–2; 37:13–19).

Does this sound familiar? This is what happens when a nation is on the verge of meeting God's active wrath. The fraudulent is usually elevated, and that which is approved is insulted. Lies are promoted above the truth, and propaganda is accepted as authentic. Conspiracies and untruths are parroted so frequently that the average bystander is bewildered, troubled, and doesn't know what to believe. When a nation or the church becomes numb to lies, that's an indication that an evil spirit has taken over. When authentic prophetic voices are muted or rejected, people tend to crave leaders who suffer from the Dunning-Kruger effect. Having learned a little, they deem themselves experts.

It's a psychological diagnosis, but the Bible has a simple name for it: pride. People suffering from this effect are incompetent and unable to recognize their own incompetence. Therefore, they have an inflated self-assessment of their abilities. When we freely accept and embrace "Thus says the Lord" statements from people God has not sent, it clearly indicates that the church has dangerously backslidden. "I did not send these prophets," declares the Lord,

> yet they have run with their message; I did not speak to them, yet they have prophesied. But if they had stood in my council, they would have proclaimed my words to my people and would have turned them from their evil ways and from their evil deeds. (Jer. 23:21–22 NIV)

This is where we are in the US today. We are in an hour in which the ways, standards, and desires of the world sit comfortably in the church. And when the idealism of the culture has postured itself within the church of the living God, then crisis, conflict, and undesirable and unexplainable hardship will shape many who long for comfort over clarity; for soothing words over sound words; for fiction over fact. We live in such a day when people are so in love with their desires that they are divorcing the ways of God to marry their own way.

Satan is answering many prayers today because he knows the hearts of men—that their ultimate aim is not the will of Christ but their own desires. But one thing I have learned about God is that the voice of his Spirit will never sacrifice clarity on the altar of popularity, unity, or compromise. Unfortunately, we tend to be drawn to and accept voices that offer comfort and convenience over voices that mandate we carry a cross. But if you are determined to find and follow the true God in this dark hour, then the cross—the old rugged one, and not the "new cross" that A. W. Tozer has written about—must be your point of reference.

Tozer once said, "The new cross does not slay the sinner, it redirects him. The old cross slew men; the new cross entertains them. The old cross condemned; the new cross amuses. The old cross destroyed confidence in the flesh; the new cross encourages it."[5]

To appear relevant and appealing to a consumer-driven audience, we have sanitized the cross to make it more suitable and tasteful to those offended by its true meaning. The modern-day cross has made life, people, one's job, and any unpleasant circumstances the issue when in reality, the true cross highlights the real issue: ourselves. When Jesus commands us to take up our cross daily, he is not referring to our wayward children, our discouraging financial status, a demanding boss, or a troubling marriage (Luke 9:23). He is talking about dying daily to ourselves because our fleshly nature seeks to dictate how we should live. Our flesh will never willingly commit suicide; it must be crucified.

May the cross that offers no apologies to the flesh, and makes no provision for the love of self, sin, and compromise, be the plumb line by which we govern our lives.

> *The cross should not just become a symbol of my private confession; it should also become the symbol of my public statement. The cross is a picture of open shame and not an advertisement for self-glorification. Too many confess the cross but their actions and beliefs contradict it.*

---

[5] From "The Old Cross and the New," by A. W. Tozer. *The Alliance Witness*, July 24, 1963.

Chapter 3

A Precursor Season: The Signs Emerge

I'm frequently asked, "Is America under judgment?" But a better question is, "What stage of judgment is America in?" In ancient Judah during the reign of Nebuchadnezzar, God's judgment was progressive but slow, allowing time for mercy to prevail. God's judgment on this country has been similar so far. Yet we should heed this warning: even the nation that housed the temple that God placed his name on experienced unthinkable consequences (Jer. 52:1–23). A people who had experienced tremendous liberty and freedom came under God's severe judgment. They crossed the Rubicon, reaching a point of no return, and devastation swiftly followed. So we have to ask ourselves: Has the US offended God so repeatedly that his cup of wrath is now full (Jer. 25:15)? Sadly, I believe we are treading toward a place and time we have never seen. We are moving from a preventable sickness to a terminal disease, and 2020 was only an initial sign of that judgment.

The year ushered in what I have coined a "precursor season." A *precursor* can be defined as a person or thing that announces or indicates the approach of something new. It shares commonality with what it precedes and often points to a future reality. The year 2020 set off an era in which God has begun to deal with things in a new way globally. Evidence of his judgment usually comes through circumstances that are challenging, mind-boggling, heartbreaking, and disheartening from a human point of view.

Precursors in Matthew 24

Matthew 24, which biblical scholars call the Olivet Discourse, describes precursors. The verses in this chapter are descriptive, prescriptive, and predictive. They depict events that took place, prescribe events that are taking place in the present and predict those that will take place in the future. Perusing the following verses can help shape your understanding of what we are seeing now and what I believe we will soon see.

Matthew 24:3–14 states:

> As He was sitting on the Mount of Olives, the disciples came to Him privately, saying, "Tell us, when will these things happen, and what will be the sign of Your coming, and of the end of the age?" And Jesus answered and said to them, "See to it that no one misleads you. For many will come in My name, saying, 'I am the Christ,' and they will mislead many people. And you will be hearing of wars and rumors of wars. See that you are not alarmed, for those things must take place, but that is not yet the end. For nation will rise against nation, and kingdom against kingdom, and there will be famines, pestilences, and earthquakes in various places. But all these things are merely the beginning of birth pains. Then they will

hand you over to tribulation and kill you, and you will be hated by all nations because of My name. And at that time many will fall away, and they will betray one another and hate one another. And many false prophets will rise up and mislead many people. And because lawlessness is increased, most people's love will become cold. But the one who endures to the end is the one who will be saved. This gospel of the kingdom shall be preached in the whole world as a testimony to all the nations, and then the end will come." (NASB)

We'll walk through some of these verses line by line to draw out a clear picture from God's point of view. Eight signs apply to and illustrate the unique time that 2020 ushered in.

At the beginning of the passage, the disciples ask Jesus two questions. (Some theologians believe they ask him three questions, but this is not our primary concern: it's the content of the questions that warrants our attention.) In reference to Jesus' mention of the temple destruction in verse two, they ask Jesus when these things will take place. They want to know when the temple will be destroyed and what the signs of his return and the end of the age will be. Jesus indirectly answers the first question by providing detailed predictions regarding the second question. Then, Jesus outlines a progression of prophetic signs that will mark his second coming.

First Sign: Deception

The first sign of Jesus' coming will be an increase in deception. Jesus warns: "See to it that no one misleads you" (Matt. 24:4). In verse five, Jesus highlights the frequency of the coming deception ("many will come in My name") and reveals that deception will prosper (many will be misled). What is deception? Or, what does it mean to be deceived? We are deceived when we believe we *know* something to be acceptable to God, but in reality, this belief has been based on our own perception and not on a clear direction. The Bible says Eve was deceived (1 Tim. 2:14), which means she believed the words of the serpent based on a false perception that caused her to devalue God's clear instructions. So, deception is a persuasive idea which causes us to believe in something that is an *un*truth based on our perception that it *is* truth. If I'm deceived, then the last person to believe I've been deceived is myself. So people who are under deception become deceptive (2 Tim. 3:13). We can understand then why Jesus was so careful to warn us to be on guard and to pay attention so we will not be misled.

The love of God is not always manifest through things he has the power to stop. Instead, on many occasions, his love is manifest in the things he allows us to endure to prepare us for what's next. For example, Christ's love for Mary and Martha did not prevent Lazarus from dying, but the word he gave them beforehand prepared them for what was to come (John 11:4). In unexpected circumstances and pain, we can have moments of weakness, and Satan can take advantage of our thoughts. But we must understand this truth about God's love: it can manifest in warnings and not always in preventions; it is reflected in restrictions and not always in permissions.

In his love, Jesus tells us to be aware of the coming deluge of deception. When Jesus says, "See to it that no one misleads you" (Matt. 24:4), he is not making a suggestion: he is voicing a command. The Greek word for "see to it," *blepo*, is not only an imperative (command) but also written in the present tense, which means it's a continual command to observe in an ongoing fashion. We can only "see to it" if we habitually put this command into practice. Staying free from deception requires obedience, humility, and continual diligence. Jesus reveals one avenue by which deception will come: "For many will come in My name, saying,

'I am the Christ, and will mislead many" (Matt. 24:5). Many wrong interpretations have caused us to misread Jesus' instructions, so let's break down verse five.

Many Will Come; Many Will Be Misled

Before describing how deception will come, Jesus highlights the severity of the coming deception. He specifies, "many will come." Here, *many* is a terrifying word. Jesus did not use the words *some* or *few*; he used the word *many*. The word describes something so great in multitude, magnitude, or quantity that it can't be numbered. Notice the certainty: he said they *will* come, not that they *might* or *may* come. He emphasizes sureness in their coming, so we shouldn't be surprised when they appear.

So, we have been warned and are commanded to be alert. But, unfortunately, herein lies a common misunderstanding and misinterpretation of the text. For years, people have quoted this verse to warn us about those who will come claiming to be the Messiah. But that's not Jesus' point. Numerous people over the centuries and others in the future will call themselves Jesus or the Messiah, but here is the question: Did they or will they deceive *many*?

Fraudulent messiah claimants might deceive a small group of people but not the masses. What Jesus tells us to watch out for is people who will come *in* his name, not *with* his name. To come in his name is to claim you represent him; to claim you are doing business or work on his behalf; to claim you are speaking on his behalf; to claim he sent you; to claim he called you to do his work. When we use this interpretation, we can see how deception will overtake many.

And what will the deceivers say? They are the Christ. *Christ* means "anointed one." They will claim they have been anointed, called, and approved to do things that heaven has not authorized. They will use God's word but alter and supplant its meaning to fit their unresolved spiritual hurt, personal pursuits, prejudices, pet theologies, and presuppositions. And the sad result? They will mislead many.

Again, Jesus emphasizes the term *will*, indicating a disturbing reality: deception is sure to increase. It will triumph and gain souls as spoil. Many will be influenced by deceptive spirits leading them down a wrong path. As they head down that path, they are prone to apostasy. This turning away from orthodox beliefs is usually gradual, and the change in one's thoughts begins to show up in one's actions. Eventually, there comes a conscious, willful abandonment of a position one previously stood by. It's a change of heart that comes from wrong thoughts.

The Problem of Apostasy

Over the last few years, a heated debate concerning what counts as apostasy has risen. So, a term that should be easily defined has come under scrutiny because the biblical definition contradicts popular theological belief systems. For example, some believe only superficial believers become subject to apostasy, for genuine believers cannot be subject to falling away. Yet, this is a preposterous view, for how could someone fall away from something they never possessed in the first place? Under this view, one might think that the fallen angels who left their proper domain were never true angels in the first place (Jude 6). But why would Christ emphasize the danger of deception in the Last Days if the danger only applied to nonbelievers? Why would Christ tell fair-weather believers to watch out for those who will misguide them if they were not genuine believers in the first place?

Beware of any theology that teaches or even implies that any repetitively warning verses in the New Testament don't apply to you. There are no such things as "hypothetical" warnings in the word of God. There is no true value in warning someone against something that's impossible of happening.

When you are convinced that you cannot fall away or be deceived, sadly, you are already deceived. Why would Satan work tirelessly to make his way into the church through erroneous teachings, unapproved leadership, worldliness, temptations, and unforgiveness, if his goal was misleading superficial believers? Such teaching is evidence of seducing spirits influencing the beliefs of many. The writer of the book of Hebrews warned true believers about the dangers of departing from God due to a hard and evil heart (Heb. 3:12–13).

How do we know if those who fall away were true believers or not? Can one's heart become hard if it was never transformed? The word *brethren* highlights the Holy Spirit's target audience. In Greek, it is *adelphos*. Depending on the context of the verse, *adelphos* is commonly used to identify Christians who share a common faith, believers united together by a common affection. Demas was called a *brother*. In his brief letter to Philemon, Paul wrote, "Epaphras, my fellow prisoner in Christ Jesus, sends you greetings. And so do Mark, Aristarchus, Demas and Luke, my fellow workers" (vv. 23–24 NIV). Demas was a believer: we know since Paul called him a fellow worker in Christ.

Demas, though, became a victim of apostasy. In his second letter to Timothy, Paul reveals that Demas deserted him: "Do your best to come to me quickly, for Demas, because he loved this world, has deserted me and has gone to Thessalonica" (2 Tim. 4:9–10 NIV). Demas worked for the Lord and walked on the right path, but the love of the world turned his heart, and he intentionally abandoned and renounced Paul and the gospel. How can the love of the world turn my heart if my heart has never forsaken the world? Demas became an apostate—he fell away—and one cannot fall away from something one never possessed or was never real.

But what about 1 John 2:19, some might wonder? "They went out from us, but they did not really belong to us. For if they had belonged to us, they would have remained with us; but their going showed that none of them belonged to us" (NIV). Using this verse to claim broadly that those who fall away were never truly saved in the first place is dangerous and misleading, for this verse has nothing to do with how many teach it and use it. Instead, this verse points out those teaching a form of Gnosticism called Docetism.

Docetism, which comes from the Greek word *dokein*, meaning "to seem," was a belief system that taught that Christ did not really come in human form and that he only seemed to have a human body like ours. This heretical teaching denied the core essentials of the gospel—Jesus' death and resurrection. If Jesus did not have a human body, he did not die. Without his death, there is no sacrifice for our sins. Without his death, there can be no resurrection. Without his resurrection, we are still in our sins (1 Cor. 15:12–17). From this context, John writes, "They went out from us, but they were not *really* of us..." (1 John 2:19 NASB). For if one does not believe that Christ came in the flesh, then that person was never saved in the first place. But if this is the only picture you have of apostasy, then chances are you have been instructed incorrectly.

Staying in the Father's Hand

If you believe that a true believer can never be deceived, then chances are you are already deceived and may be deceiving others. But what about John 10:29, where Jesus claims that no one can pluck believers from the Father's hand? Some mistakenly think Jesus is promising that a believer's salvation is unconditionally secured. However, the issue is not believers' eternal security but whether that security is conditional or unconditional. Jesus said,

> I have already told you, and you don't believe me. The proof is the work I do in my Father's name. But you don't believe me because you are not my sheep.

> My sheep listen to my voice; I know them, and they follow me. I give them eternal life, and they will never perish. No one can snatch them away from me, for my Father has given them to me, and he is more powerful than anyone else. No one can snatch them from the Father's hand. The Father and I are one. (John 10:25–30 NLT)

Many proclaim the great promise in this verse but overlook its conditions. You cannot proclaim to have eternal life that no one can take away because of the Father's power to protect you, mentioned in verses 28 and 29, but skip over the requirement in verse 27 of listening to and following Jesus who knows you. In Greek, the verbs for *listen*, *know*, and *follow* in verse 27 are in the present tense. They point to habitual and continuous actions, which therefore reflect a consistent lifestyle. When these present-tense verbs are combined with the indicative mood in this passage, they represent something that's contemporaneous in action, as opposed to action that took place in the past or only the present. Understanding this verse through the lens of Greek helps us understand Jesus is saying that eternal security belongs to those who continually hear, follow, and obey him.

So, what happens to those who stop hearing, following, and obeying? It's like what the apostle Peter describes in his last epistle: They return to former vomit and wallow in the mire (see 2 Pet. 2:20–22). But what about the promise in Romans 8:39 that "nothing will be able to separate us from the love of God" (NIV)? While all of Romans 8 is encouraging and edifying to the believer, it's important to understand the context of this powerful chapter. Many teach verses 31–39 as if they pertain to salvation and therefore reach wrong conclusions. These verses do not refer to salvation but to suffering. Paul cheers on believers who face hardship and suffering due to their salvation, and he encourages us to press on through tough times because our suffering will not separate us from God's love.

Therefore, just because we suffer doesn't mean Christ has stopped loving us. Admittedly, going through lengthy and painful hardships can cause us to question Christ's love. However, it's uplifting to know that nothing in this world nor the enemy of our faith can do anything to move us from that starting block. While Paul does not list it here, one thing can separate us from God: sin (see Isa. 59:1–2). So to reiterate, the concept that nothing can separate us from the love of Christ should be taught in reference to hardships the believer faces, not salvation.

Second Sign: Spiritual Deviation

The first sign, spiritual deception, precedes the second sign: *spiritual deviation*. When you see deviation from what's true via a contradiction in one's spiritual life—applauding and agreeing with things that are true on the one hand but also promoting and supporting things that are associated with a lie on the other hand—it is an indicator that deceptive spirits are in operation in that person's life. We are living in times in which people feel justified and empowered by their beliefs, in the present, that contradicts their former. Like King David, who once declared in Psalm 84:10, "I would rather be a doorkeeper in the house of my God than dwell in the tents of the wicked" (NIV); many once confessed this statement but now have drifted from this view. Many now see church as optional, and even repulsive. I call this sort of thinking, the "slippery slope syndrome." It's when people start to erect and substitute a self-willed opinion in the place of a previous upheld truth, and now, selectively choose what they want to believe, while acting absent-minded to former confessions. This deviation is spiritually contagious and will lead to dangerous grounds. It is much like walking on frozen ice. One's footing may seem solid and secure until the ground underneath them starts to crack and one realizes that they were walking and trusting in a false reality. How far can one deviate before the ice breaks and it leads to a spiritual drowning? Spiritual deviation involves demonic persuasion; therefore, it is not something that should be overlooked, for it is an alarming concern. We don't like to deviate alone because it tends to highlight our failures to others. So we look for those who will join us on this course to justify our current condition.

Jesus proceeds to move toward the ongoing "hearing of wars and the rumors of wars" in Matthew 24 verse 6 to encourage believers that while these things must happen, they do not signal the end, so we shouldn't be shaken or disturbed. This verse is important because he is connecting the things that must happen to the next signs.

What Must Happen

The word *must* in Greek is *dei*. The word describes something as inevitable and necessary; therefore, it should not be overlooked. In scripture, the term is broken down into three categories, used in three particular ways to mean unchangeable, redeeming, and compelling. For example, when Jesus began to explain the things he would have to face, he used the word *must* to show that his suffering and death were unchangeable (Matt. 16:21). When he explained he *must* go through Samaria, it indicated he was on a divine mission to bring redemption to the woman at the well (John 4:4). When John the Baptizer said that Christ *must* increase, but he *must* decrease (see John 3:25–30), he was declaring that his will was to surrender to the will of God. So, when Jesus uses *must* (*dei*) to say that "*those things* [wars and rumors of wars] must take place," he declares that the signs are not only necessary but unchangeable (Matt. 24:6).

Jesus continues explaining the subsequent signs that must happen. We can't pray them away; we can't fast enough to make them disappear; we cannot do enough good deeds to avoid them. Despite how unpleasant, unfair, or uncomfortable these things will be, he tells us they must happen. Therefore, if we are going to walk in a manner that pleases God, we must make appropriate adjustments to our wills and mindsets.

Dangers of Deviation Due to Disapproval

Christians have become mouthpieces for conspiracy theories and unbiblical, self-centered rhetoric simply because they are personally at odds with how signs are manifesting. In other words, they are more focused on how the signs are formed or created than on the purpose or intention of the signs themselves. That inappropriate focus leads to the propagation of dangerous narratives. And many Christians were and are conduits of propaganda and conspiracy theories regarding COVID-19's origin and the COVID vaccine's efficacy and purpose. But making statements that the virus is a hoax is irresponsible and has led to ungodly actions that hinder the church's ability to evangelize. Who will listen to such rhetoric when they've lost loved ones to COVID? I see such speech as an enemy to salvation. So despite any controversy as to how the virus formed, the issue and others like it should never be allowed to overshadow the warnings Christ has spoken. There is biblical precedent for this position.

For example, when Jesus set in motion to tell his disciples the signs that would lead to his death, Peter disapproved of what Jesus was saying. And Peter then became an oracle for the voice of Satan (Matt. 16:21–23). Like Peter, we can unknowingly become proponents of evil, even though the things we see are evidence of heaven speaking. Consider the COVID-19 situation: it was bad, and it still is. It has led to the belief that the vaccine developed for COVID was designed to depopulate the culture, and now in its wake even other vaccinations are seen as bad, including all those for infants. Some believe it is the mark of the beast. Christians and owners of Christian television stations are pushing such damaging narratives. We see the hypocrisy of the situation in stories about President Trump's supporters who followed his lead against the shot, not knowing he was vaccinated, which helped his recovery from COVID. People become so focused on where COVID came from that they overlook the biblical message that plagues must happen. Jesus never told us how they will form, nor did he say that should be our focus.

Keep in mind this truth: God can allow things to happen that are completely contrary to his nature to bring his ultimate purpose to pass—just ask Job (see Job 1:1–22; 42:1–17; cf. James 5:11). God is emphatically against murder but allowed murder to be the means of his Son's death to fulfill his plan (Acts 2:22–24; 5:29–32). I'm not implying that we should be dismissive of unfairness and wrongness. Still, I'm concerned that unbridled emotions lead to impulsiveness, which can undermine and suffocate us so much that we will find ourselves at odds with the wisdom of God and therefore miss the intended purpose for such acts (Job 38:1–3).

Third Sign: Social Disorder

Christ gives us the next group of signs in Matthew 24:7—"nation will rise against nation." The word *nation* in Greek is *ethnos*, from which we get the English word *ethnic*. It means a distinct people group and a particular culture. Once again, don't overlook the word *will* in this verse. It's amazing how people can take every precaution to be prepared for a probability but show little desire to be prepared for an assurance. We need to take serious heed here because Jesus is declaring certainties, not possibilities. Jesus is telling us that ethnic groups will rise up against one another, which defines our third sign—*social disorder*.

A very interesting story developed before the days of King Asa's reforms. Second Chronicles 15 tells how Israel had gone a long time without the true God, without a true priest, and without the law. The people had become content and satisfied with a false god, misleading priests, and a fabricated law. Verses 5 and 6 reveal there was no peace in the land and recount that great turmoil was the headline of the day. Next, we see a profound state of affairs: nation was against nation and city against city, for God—not Satan—troubled them with all kinds of adversity. Sound familiar? Notice that because of the sin of the people who were supposed to be following and serving God, God allowed adversity to arise amongst ethnic groups and that adversity created disorder in the culture.

Social disorder is disturbing to behold because the majority will always be in a position to help push the narrative surrounding it. The imbalance of power will produce injustice and other evil workings on many levels. Nevertheless, despite the unfairness, this is one of the signs that Christ warned us must happen. God will allow injustice in the land to highlight injustice among his own people. God will highlight racism within a culture to highlight that same evil among his own people. He will highlight social elitism to expose the partiality that exists among his own (James 2:1–9). He will highlight the greed and the covetousness in the culture to reveal the self-centeredness of his own people. The hypocrisy among believers is that we show great passion for issues outside the church, but we are silent when those same issues plague the church from within. I'm not saying we shouldn't defend the cause of those with no voice, but God will not bypass the church to fix the world. Judgment does not begin in the culture; it starts in the house of God (1 Pet. 4:17).

When David committed adultery with Bathsheba and orchestrated a plan to kill her husband, God waited many months to deal with David's sin. When God was ready, he sent the prophet Nathan to deliver a parable to David (2 Sam. 12:1–15). The parable highlights the injustice, unfairness, and cruelty of a rich man misusing his power and authority to seize a poor man's only sheep. Once David heard the story, he rose up with great indignation and declared that such a man repay the poor man four times what he had stolen. David didn't realize that the story of injustice and unfairness was about him. God used a cultural story of unfairness to highlight David's sin and hypocrisy, and he does the same with his church today.

Fourth Sign: International Disputes

Next, Jesus, in the same verse (Matt. 24:7), moves on to kingdom against kingdom. In modern terminology, we would say countries will rise up against other countries for political posturing and power. This is the fourth sign—*international disputes*. Countries will begin to exert their political and military might to position themselves aggressively against other weaker countries. This is necessary to realign the power of nations to fulfill end-time prophecies. In case you didn't know, the US is not mentioned in Bible prophecies, which likely means that eventually, this country will lose its influence among other nations. And countries usually lose their influence when they can no longer fix or solve their own problems. During Christ's first coming, the power of the nations shifted from the East to the West, and Rome was in power. But at his second coming, the opposite will take place, and the power of the nations will shift from the West back to the East (Ezek. 38:1–6). In years to come, we will see strong countries in the West start to look weak due to a lack of stability and deterioration from within.

Fifth Sign: Physical Destruction

Then Christ mentions the fifth sign—*physical destruction*. He warns of coming famines, pestilences, and earthquakes. I call this sign "physical destruction" because the three causes not only physical damage but also the loss of life. Notice they are referred to in the plural, not singular, form to show their frequency and severity as Christ's return approaches.

Let's focus on pestilences. The Greek is *loimos*, which means plagues. It's described as a contagious bacterial disease that becomes a public menace, a threat and a danger to the community. In this country alone, COVID-19 has become the deadliest plague in history, surpassing the deadly Spanish flu of 1918. A country that prides itself on its technology and medical acumen has struggled to gain control over this disease. I thank God for modern medicine, but modern medicine cannot override prophecy. What we are seeing played out among us regarding COVID-19 must come to pass. I will repeat this again: often, we get so wrapped up in the means or method of what is happening that we can't see the root of why it's happening. Maintaining a micro view can lead to superficial and meaningless disputes.

Whether you did or didn't believe in the vaccine, it's undeniable that countless lost their lives to propaganda—by believing this plague was just a hoax or was man-made to control the masses. But such talking points should never be the focus of true, biblical Christians because we are supposed to be driven by that which is honest, prophetic, scriptural, true, and factual—not by lies, social media commentary, political talking points, and personal preferences. The dissemination of disinformation does not come from the Ancient of Days but from the god of this age. From scripture, we know plagues will become more frequent and extremely deadly as we get closer to Christ's return, and there is nothing we can do in the grand scheme of things to stop them. But we are called to make appropriate and practical adjustments when the signs appear.

In Matthew 24:8, Jesus begins with the word *but*, as he presents a contrast to what he just said. When *but* is used at the beginning of a verse, it's designed to get us to slow down because we are entering an intersection of thought. The word *but* is like hinges on a door. They are designed to swing open to cause us to enter into something new. Jesus continues after *but* with *all these things*. What are "all these things"? They are the things he just mentioned. They are "*merely* the beginning of birth pangs." What are birth pangs from a scriptural point of view? Hebrew prophets frequently used labor pains as a figure of the Last Days and of God's coming judgment. A woman does not have labor pains at the beginning of her pregnancy, for labor pains are not a sign of conception but a sign of approaching delivery. And as the frequency and the intensity of those pangs will increase until the baby is born, so will these signs. They will grow in frequency and intensity until the appointed time, the return of Christ.

Christ proceeds from the ills of the culture to the ills of the church. Now, in his love, he prepares his followers for what will happen to some and what will take place among those who call upon his name. He mentions our sixth, seventh, and eighth signs—*spiritual discrimination, spiritual disruption, and spiritual disunity.* In verses 9 through 12, Christ uses the word *then*. The term is significant because it implies an expression of time. The sequence of the next three verses work in unison. Christ becomes more explicit about the spiritual challenges believers must deal with to prepare for troublesome and disheartening times.

Sixth Sign: Spiritual Discrimination

Jesus first warns the disciples about the *discrimination* that his followers will suffer. Many of our brothers and sisters will be handed over to authorities to be persecuted, and many will be killed because of their faith and trust in Christ. Notice that Jesus does not hide what it will cost believers to serve him. He openly and clearly says that physical death at the hands of others will be the allotment for many who serve him. And he also mentions something that could not have been a first-century problem. We know that believers suffered great harm by the religious hands of the first-century Jewish system and Ancient Rome, but Christ says something futuristic—that believers will be "hated by all nations" (Matt. 24:9). This particular word *hated* in Greek is *miseo*. It means to dislike someone or something to the point that you find it or them detestable. It is a premeditated hate that will cause one to pursue someone in vindictive anger. It is also used in the present tense, which means a hatred that's continual or habitual. Jesus prophetically speaks of a global hatred against his followers.

Some interpret the hatred as directed at the nation of Israel and not the church, and I'm not trying to discredit that interpretation or to teach Replacement Theology—an erroneous doctrine that teaches that the church has replaced God's chosen people. But the text can apply to Christians. Over the last decade, we have seen a great hatred for the gospel and the standards of Christ among nations. It seems like other religions can freely promote their god without resistance, but when Christians mention certain aspects of Jesus and his ways, it has become treated as hate speech.[1] Discrimination against tenets of the Christian faith will steadily intensify as we get closer to Christ's second coming.

Seventh Sign: Spiritual Disruption

Jesus has been teaching about the external hardships that believers will face, and he moves into the internally destructive behavior that is running and will run rampant inside the body of Christ. Jesus prophetically addresses the root cause of the spiritual disruption that, unfortunately, will happen among believers. He highlights the deluge of offense that will lead to more collateral damage: "And at that time many will fall away, and they will betray one another and hate each other" (Matt. 24:10). It's been rightly said by many that today's US culture is one of

---

[1] For examples, see James Duvall's "New Statistics on Growing Persecution Against Christians," *The Liberty Champion*, December 6, 2022, https://www.liberty.edu/champion/2022/12/new-statistics-on-growing-persecution-against-christians/.

the most easily offended cultures in centuries. We are oversensitive in our emotions yet hypersensitive to the truth; therefore, we are insensitive and desensitized to hearing the voice of the Spirit. This has opened the door to a post-truth era in which personal feelings, beliefs, and biases are elevated above what is objectively factual and biblically sound. Notice that being offended will also produce and lead to more unsettling sins like betraying and hating one another. Our lack of spiritual maturity will result in our undisciplined behavior being hijacked and taken captive by Satan, who will create deep conflict among brothers and sisters.

The Problem With Offense

The Greek for "offended" is *skandalízō*. Depending on the context of the verse, this word has a variety of definitions. It's commonly defined as placing a stumbling block in a person's way to entrap them or entice them to sin. It also means to cause a person to begin to distrust and depart from one whom he ought to trust. It means to fall away from something once trusted and obeyed. It means to be offended by another because one sees something one disapproves of, which hinders one from acknowledging and respecting the other person. Does this sound familiar?

We are so easily offended in the church these days that anything that ruffles our feathers and goes counter to our feelings, opinions, and desires, we now label as traumatizing, abuse, unjust, legalistic, or archaic. The tendency to be offended is so out of control that Satan has even convinced us that sound doctrine is unkind. The same word that helped bring us out of sin is now viewed as unacceptable, unloving, and ungodly. That which we used to have such an appetite for now seems repulsive and primitive. We will almost accept anything that sounds godly if it feels caring and loving.

The Loss of Teaching in Favor of Coaching

Not only as an itinerant speaker but also a pastor, I've seen people transition away from having a healthy appetite for sound doctrine to preferring teaching that only reinforces their personal wishes. Many no longer have the same tolerance or endurance for wholesome teachings or even biblical counseling they previously delighted in. Today, people prefer to be coached rather than taught. What is the difference? When someone prefers coaching, they already have in their heart a predetermined course of action toward a goal they want to achieve. Therefore, they search for and gather around themselves individuals who will show them how to achieve that desired outcome—essentially, they seek cheerleaders who will make them feel good about their progress, no matter what that progress looks like. Coaching like this is foundationally different from teaching or Spirit-led counseling.

> *People often resort to alternatives when leaders are afraid to proclaim standards.*

In contrast, when an individual has knowledge they'd like to attain, a particular belief they'd like to better understand, or another desire they'd like to achieve, if they are open to being taught, they will seek wise counsel concerning what would be proper. While being counseled by a teacher, the individual will often conclude that their original desire is not in harmony with God's desire for them (Prov. 19:20–21). Rather than taking offense at the teacher's instructions, they realize that God's way is the best and are then willing to forsake their plan for God's will.

Paul warned us that in the Last Days, men and women will no longer have a desire to tolerate or to put up with sound instructions (2 Tim. 4:1–5). While on this note, I believe it's imperative for us to understand that Paul could not have been speaking in reference to unbelievers in this verse, for since when have unbelievers ever desired to hear sound teaching? He revealed what the actions of such people will look like: "They will follow their own desires and will look for teachers who will tell them whatever their itching ears want to hear" (v. 3 NLT). As the sad result of such tragedy, he explains, "They will reject the truth and chase after myths" (v. 4). How do you reach a generation who favors life coaches over Spirit-appointed leadership?

"Blessed is he who is not offended"

Many have shunned proclaiming the true gospel message to avoid offending listeners. Yet the gospel in itself is offensive (1 Cor. 1:23). Jesus never changed his message to massage people's egos. He never catered to humankind's self-esteem. He never allowed cultural relevance to alter his mission. When you have a culture that thinks with their feelings and listens with their eyes, being offended is inevitable. A tidal wave of offense has swept through the body of Christ in such a way that it has produced a great *spiritual disruption* in people's relationship with God and with each other. If my vertical relationship with God is impacted, it will show up in my horizontal relationship with others. Satan has successfully derailed and uprooted divine relationships through offense and unresolved conflict. Anything heaven approves must overcome the deceptive schemes of Satan to continue to thrive, for he works tirelessly to disjoin what God has merged together. Also, many have become so offended by God on a variety of issues that even the mention of his name makes them angry.

Some feel it's worthless to suffer for the gospel's sake while the wicked still prosper (Ps. 73:1–28). Some, because they felt like God did not answer their prayers when their loved ones suffered death at the hands of COVID-19, believe that he can no longer be trusted. Feeling like God let you down or did not meet your expectations can produce an offended heart. And when one's heart is offended by God, it moves them to start developing unsound and improper thoughts (Prov. 18:19). When one's thought life becomes dishonorable to God, it will eventually lead to a mindset that's attractive and suitable to demonic activity.

We see this progression in the life of John the Baptist: a man whom Gabriel—an angel who stands in the literal presence of God—announced his arrival (Luke 1:5–19); a man who was filled with the Spirit from birth (Luke 1:15); a man whose purpose was prophetically spoken 700 years before he came on the scene (Isa. 40:3; Luke 3:3–6); a man chosen by God to identify the Lamb of God (John 1:29); a man who had the testimony that he was the only person in human history to baptize Jesus, God in the flesh (Matt. 3:13–17). Nevertheless, near the end of his life, John nearly stumbled because Christ did not meet his expectations (Matt. 11:1–11).

If Satan almost moved John to become offended, how much more vulnerable are we? Jesus' message to John is the same message he gives us today: "Blessed is he who is not offended because of me" (Matt. 11:6 NKJV). What exactly does this mean? It means that if you truly desire to honor and wholeheartedly submit to the will of the Lord, there will be plenty of opportunities for you to be troubled and displeased by him. There will be moments when you will be upset and disheartened by his words, his ways, his desires, and his timing (Isa. 55:8–9). There will be moments when you will disapprove of what seems to be a lack of action or response on his behalf: but blessed are you if none of these things shake your confidence and trust in who Christ is. In the words of the late Vance Havner, who paraphrased the text: "Blessed is the man who doesn't get upset by the way I run my business."[2] That's what Jesus was saying to John. "Happy are you if you don't get upset by the way I do my business." May we take heed like John, and many others in the scriptures, who model what it looks like to trust in a God who will never

---

[2] Quoted in "The Forgotten Beatitude," by Dan Cler. *Old Paths Musings*, August 31, 2016. http://oldpathsbaptistchurch.com/the-forgotten-beatitude/.

lose control of the plans he has for our lives, even though we might not agree with or understand everything that's happening.

Overcoming Offense

Learning how to overcome offense is paramount. Not maturing spiritually in the Last Days will make one a victim of and a conduit for ungodly counsel, betrayal, and hate (2 Sam. 15:12; 16:15–23; 17:21–23). Notice that Satan is strategic in his attack. The root is being offended, and he knows once a person has fallen into this trap, the outcome will be—not will perhaps be or might be—it *will for certain* be betrayal and hate. In Greek, the word for betrayal is *paradidomi*. It describes willingly handing over something or someone into the hands of another power. Once a person becomes offended, they don't mind giving a person over into the hands or into the opinions of others, which will produce unsettling animosity among brothers and sisters. Betrayal can hide while you are serving, but it stands out when things don't go your way. A heart of betrayal will create an illogical mind. It was the obedience of Mary that exposed the heart of Judas (John 12:1–6). He despised Mary not because she had a spiritual title but because she was selfless and submitted. A betraying heart hates and ridicules a submissive spirit. It misdiagnoses a submissive person as being under control but will consider betrayal a form of spiritual freedom.

There is another truth concerning Judas and his vindictive heart: he was willing to betray Christ because, in his own warped mind, it seemed like he was being offered more for the betrayal than he was being offered for submitting to God's agenda (Mark 24:10-11). A betraying heart will always choose what it can gain over that which it feels can no longer offer any value. This type of hate produces a strong negative reaction toward a person's name, and it denotes a devoted resentment that arises when someone feels injured by the actions of another.

Eighth Sign: Spiritual Disunity

The global hatred Christ warned about in Matthew 24 verse 9 will now find a home among believers. Internal hatred can produce such a volatile environment in the church that it disrupts the unity of the believers. Mark these words down: Whenever there is *spiritual disunity* in a church, it will open a door to a false spokesperson. Satan will raise up someone who will proclaim or announce false utterances under the pretense that the Holy Spirit is speaking to them. And Satan intends for some among the body of believers to believe such fabricated prophecies, which will lead many away from the right course and into deception (Matt. 24:11).

We've seen such things when churches go through a split. Because someone desires, at the moment, to be acknowledged and highlighted, through pride, they become an instrument of Satan, and they deceive others. I heard a story recently of a church going through a schism. A particular person, charismatic in appearance and jovial in his presentation, pulled away over a thousand members from this previous ministry to start his own church, only to stop pastoring them less than five years later. I wonder what happened to the people who followed him.

Satan will lead you down a road that seems right in the moment, only for you to find out later that you have been bewitched and led astray. Sadly, once disunity like this is in the church, it's hard to remove it. So Satan will continue to generate strife until many walk away from it all, for that is the end game in his scheme.

Lawlessness and Cold Hearts

Christ tells us that because of lawlessness, the love of many will be extinguished (Matt. 12:24). In a climate of suspicion and dissension, the word of God and obedience to his word will usually take a back seat to anger, strong-willed opinions, and quarrels. Here is one truth that we need to understand biblically because otherwise, it sounds oxymoronic: Christ is not fond of division in his body, but when discord is happening among believers, it allows the church to see who really lives by the word of God and who lives by their own viewpoints (1 Cor. 11:18–19). Jesus tells us that people's love for one another will grow cold, and they will become less devoted to spiritual matters because of lawlessness. Once again, Jesus is not speaking to unbelievers who "believe" in word only.

When have unbelievers' hearts not been cold? How can a heart turn cold when cold is all it has ever known? The word for lawlessness in Greek is *anomia*. It means people who live like God has not given them a word. It's to disregard the authority of God and his established authority among men. It's an attitude that rejects what God has spoken and couldn't care less what people think. It's an attitude that replaces God's word with personal desires. It's an attitude that cannot be restrained or governed by God's word. It's an attitude that believes that rules and structures are forms of legalism and control, not influenced by grace, and hence should be outright rejected. In essence, the root of all lawlessness is rebellion. Therefore, for many, their love of God, for people and for the things associated with God will grow dim. It's difficult to love others when self-rule becomes one's sole priority for living. The desire and fire that many once had will be extinguished due to a coldness or hardness of the heart. Abusing one's freedom as a believer and the presence of unresolved conflict can numb one's affection toward others and the church, which is indeed Satan's objective (Gal. 5:13–15).

Rebellion Leads to Judgment

What is spiritual rebellion? Rebellion is open hostility and opposition to God's word and his established order. It is more lethal than deception, for deception is only the vehicle. In Satan's kingdom, deception is the means of transportation, rebellion is the action of the transportation, and destruction is the end result of that transportation. Satan knows from personal experience that God's holiness will not condone rebellion. It is not something to take lightly. Throughout the Bible, rebellion was always followed by God's judgment, and his judgment was always severe (2 Chron. 26:16–21).

In the creation story, God made man, then woman, and gave them dominion over creatures (Gen. 1:27–29). That was God's ordained and prescribed order. But when sin entered humanity, the creature influenced the woman, she then influenced the man, and the man then dishonored God (Gen. 3:1–19). The order and authorized authority of God's will were reversed and turned upside down through disobedience. Why? Because everything Satan touches has rebellion written all over it.

What do Satan, Adam, and Cain have in common? They all represent a first. Satan was the first angel to rebel against God. Adam was the first man to rebel against God. Cain was the firstborn man to rebel against God. Moreover, there is another frightening thing they have in common—they all received the same verdict from God: expulsion. All three were discharged, dismissed, and removed from a place God intended them to function in. This is the consequence of rebellion.

The Ultimate Judgment: Spiritual Abandonment

We often assess the judgment of God in terms of the loss of physical things, but the most severe form of judgment is spiritual abandonment by God. When God removes you from an intended place or thing by allowing you to become a spiritual vagabond, this is the most damaging judgment (Gen. 4:16). What causes one to become a spiritual vagabond? When a person's life becomes void of any authentic spiritual activity, they become restless in their spirit, which influences them to move from place to place; and move from one thing to the next without establishing any spiritual fruit. The constant wandering is evidence of a life that lacks true spiritual insight. As a result, the person is always on the move without any fixed destination. Moreover, this is the irony of being judged spiritually that commonly brings a spiritual delusion: God can evict someone spiritually, but he or she may still be accumulating earthly wealth and honor.

Consider this: Satan left heaven with more than he had in his beginning; Adam left the garden with more than he had in the beginning, and Cain is removed from the presence of God with an accumulated knowledge of evil and the skills for urbanization (Gen. 4:17). God can expel you from your authorized place, but you may still possess and achieve things. Satan was removed and built an evil kingdom; Adam was removed and had a wife and started a sinful bloodline; Cain was removed and built a city that cultivated rebellion. Mark this down: In his kingdom, Satan doesn't mind rewarding the rebellious with the things of this world because rebellion is a badge of honor in his domain. But there is a difference between God's blessings and Satan's rewards. Don't be deceived. If Satan offered the King of Glory fame and the things of this world if he would only veer from his Father's plans (Matt. 4:8–10), how much more will he attempt to mislead us? It is alarming to hear sermons and read books that offer believers what Satan offered Christ in the wilderness. So, pay attention in these Last Days to what you hear and read. Be careful of any teaching that offers you earthly results apart from God's appointed process.

Problematic Pragmatism

It's necessary here to highlight the philosophy of pragmatism, a flawed belief system (Col. 2:8). It upholds the idea that the end justifies the means. A believer who governs their life with pragmatism believes God is behind every success because of the outcome. This believer says, "If something works, it must be God." But just because something worked doesn't always mean God is behind it. Pragmatism, in this sense, offers no true root system. It's moveable, therefore unreliable, and it shifts all over the place depending on how the winds of culture blow. The winds of the culture are as strong as the winds of the world that help ships reach their destination, but the culture winds have never directed people toward God. Who would build their life on shifting sand? Pragmatism may get you applauded by this world, but the end results will find you spiritually delusional, empty, and lost. The fall of Willow Creek Community Church, based in Chicago, provides an example. Due to its fantastic, quick growth in numbers of attendees (2017 marked 25,000 members), many evangelical churches followed their pattern, which was essentially based on a business model of pleasing customers. But to see what's happened there now, including sexual misconduct scandals, it's pretty embarrassing.[3] And even during the height of their growth, a church evaluation revealed the majority of those who had attended for years had not progressed in their spiritual growth. So while it looked like God provided direction, on further inspection, we see the model was based on pragmatism and worldliness and was not God-inspired.

Rebellion is indeed spiritual, as it originated from Satan (a supernatural being), but it's not always godly. Great shame will be the harvest of those who walk in rebellion but are convinced they are heaven bound. What will be a driving force of disunity and dwindling love in the Last Days? The same thing that caused a split in heaven and drew one-third of the angels: rebellion—Satan-inspired disobedience.

Rebellion can bring people to such a twisted and distorted state that it convinces them that they can dismiss the standards and order of God

---

[3] See articles like the following: Warren Cole Smith, "Guest Post: What Happened at Willow Creek?," *The Roys Report*, February 24, 2021, https://julieroys.com/guest-post-what-happened-at-willow-creek/.
"Willow Creek Church Is Laying off 30 Percent of Its Staff," *RELEVANT*, May 20, 2022, https://relevantmagazine.com/faith/church/willow-creek-church-is-laying-off-30-percent-of-its-staff/.
"Willow Creek Repents?," *CT: Christianity Today*, October 18, 2007, https://www.christianitytoday.com/pastors/2007/october-online-only/willow-creek-repents.html.

and not adhere to what God has spoken and established. Yet they will believe that when they die, God will welcome them into his domain. However, ungodly rebellion is a sign of disunity that opens the door to false teaching. In Ephesians 4, Paul admonishes us to endeavor to keep the unity. Notice he said *keep*, not *create*. God has never instructed us to be creative in establishing unity. If we have to try to program unity, our efforts will eventually derail us into personal disagreements that can cause disunity with others and with him. Keeping the unity that God has commanded and preserved will be a fight, for Satan knows the uniqueness of God's blessing and the strength of brothers and sisters yoked together in biblical unity. He knows a kingdom divided cannot stand and will try to exploit that. However, there is a bond of peace in unity that exists that our adversary is terrified of. So despite differences we have in personalities, may we fight for true unity of being one in purpose.

Conclusion

These are the eight signs that must occur: *spiritual deception, spiritual deviation, social disorder, international disputes, physical destruction, spiritual discrimination, spiritual disruption,* and *spiritual disunity*. To be obedient to the command to "keep the unity," not to recreate unity (Eph. 4:1–3), we must observe the conditions of culture and understand how to discern the signs of the times developing in the culture. A failure to discern these will leave us vulnerable and defenseless to an antagonistic enemy who can't be seen, and neither does he die. Our only help is in our Lord and in his word, which is our responsibility to apply (Eph. 6:10–13).

It's not uncommon for us to periodically see several of the eight signs in Matthew 24 throughout a year. But what made 2020 such a unique and prophetically significant year was that all these signs began to happen at once. All eight signs revealed themselves at the same time to show us that we have entered into a different time period with God. The intensity of hostility is all around us, and Christ will not stop what he has warned us is coming. Leading up to the return of Christ, deception and lying spirits will greatly intensify. In Jewish teaching, there is a phrase, *Kal va-homer*, meaning light and heavy. Kal va-homer is an exegetical principle that assumes that what applies in a lenient case inescapably applies in a stricter case. For our purposes, deception has always been around (light), so how much more will it be intensified in these latter times (heavy)? Seducing spirits and their temptations will be the driving force for hostility within and for the great end time apostasy (2 Thess. 2:3). The Bible does not promise a great harvest of souls coming into the church, but it does declare a great falling away.

Chapter 4

The Foundation of Hostility

In times of crisis, confusion, frustration, and disappointment, only two things are essential to a believer—knowing God's timing and having God's perspective. This is not something you learn from reading books alone: you learn it from studying the scriptures and by walking with the Lord. Matthew 16:1–4 says,

> Then the Pharisees and Sadducees came, and testing Him asked that He would show them a sign from heaven. He answered and said to them, "When it is evening you say, 'It will be fair weather, for the sky is red'; and in the morning, 'It will be foul weather today, for the sky is red and threatening.' Hypocrites! You know how to discern the face of the sky, but you cannot discern the signs of the times. A wicked and adulterous generation seeks after a sign, and no sign

shall be given to it except the sign of the prophet Jonah." And He left them and departed. (NKJV)

The Pharisees and Sadducees did not get along due to differences in their political and spiritual ideologies. But when Jesus showed up, they put their differences aside, recognizing that they had a common foe—Christ. The Pharisees were leaders of the synagogue and considered the spiritual leaders in ancient Israel, while the Sadducees were leaders over the temple and used religion to support their political agenda. The Sadducees were like political activists. Jesus referred to both parties as hypocrites, also known as spiritual pretenders.

Neither sought God's perspective or timing: they preferred miraculous signs. When we are driven to weigh authenticity via signs, we open ourselves up to be led astray. I'm not saying God won't ever drop nuggets to point you in a direction or confirm his will with something supernatural. However, we need to be careful not to elevate the miraculous over the word of God. Satan can also produce and work signs (2 Thess. 2:9). The Pharisees and Sadducees were missing what Christ was saying, yet they still asked him for signs.

It's easy to learn intellectually of God's ways and still not know them. We don't just need to learn about his ways; we also need to experience them. What we learn has to be lived. Otherwise, we can have scriptural knowledge yet be deficient in knowing God's timing and perspective. For example, the Pharisees were skilled in knowledge of Hebrew scriptures. Some were even considered experts in the law (John 3:1). They were not juvenile or ignorant. They had all the verses, yet they could not discern God's timing or perspective. Their spiritual awareness was so inadequate that they failed to prepare the people. Therefore, Jesus wept over the city for their negligence in recognizing God's divine moment (Luke 19:41–44).

Simply having intellectual information does not mean you are in right standing with God. A.W. Tozer once said, "To be entirely safe from the devil's snares the man of God must be completely obedient to the Word of the Lord. The driver on the highway is safe, not when he reads the signs, but when he obeys them. So it is with the Scriptures. To be effective, they must be obeyed."[1] Revelation is necessary for our transformation, but revelation without application is just intellectual stimulation. And intellectual stimulation apart from application will hinder true transformation.

Make no mistake: The believer's life is marked by dilemmas, crises, and crossroads. The will of God is not something you add to your life. You either intentionally choose it or intentionally reject it (Luke 7:30). Choosing to follow the will of God is not like picking out a particular color of car from the dealership. The will of God pertains to your whole life. Satan knows depths of the will of God that we are not aware of. So when we reach crossroads in our lives, we need to determine what God desires. This is why knowing God's timing and perspective is essential. The Tower of Babel can seem acceptable until God comes down (Gen. 11:7–9). The people building it shared a false sense of unity, which seemed acceptable because of the initial results of their efforts. But all of that means nothing until God comes down. And we know what happened—the people were scattered and confused, and the tower was abolished. Satan will allow you to build a skyscraper and have you thinking God is behind what you are doing until his sovereignty appears. The will of God is not always about results—but it will always be about obedience.

Keep in mind, in the book of John, miracles are referred to as *signs* because Jesus' miracles point people toward God. A sign is invalid if it's not pointing you in the right direction (John 2:11). Jesus wasn't against signs: he was against performing signs for people who were still not going to believe. These kinds of people are part of a wicked and

---

[1] A.W. Tozer, "Feeding on God's Word in Obedience and Humility," from *Morning and Evening with A.W. Tozer,* Evening Devotional for January 21, 2022. Bible Portal. https://bibleportal.com/devotional/morning-evening-aw-tozer/feeding-on-gods-word-in-obedience-and-humility.

adulterous generation. Second Chronicles 18 is a prophetic picture of what the body of Christ at large looks like from heaven's perspective. Eight characters in this scene reflect traits of personalities that currently operate in the body of Christ. There are Ahab, Jehoshaphat, the false prophets, Micaiah, the people, Zedekiah, the lying spirit, and God. What we see in this chapter is apocalyptic—it is something happening behind the curtain in heaven that humanity cannot see unless God makes it known. *Apocalypse* refers to something being uncovered. It's when the veil is being lifted, and we see this in 2 Chronicles 18. Things had reached such a tragic end that God allowed a lie to deliver his plan of judgment on the earth.

The Hatred That Breeds Hostility

Hostility, also known as enmity, is a deep-rooted hatred. It stems from a carnal mind. If your mind is set on the flesh, it will breed hostility and death (Rom. 8:5–7). The COVID-19 pandemic has exposed hatred that was not only concealed in the hearts of people outside the church but also in the hearts of those within. Anger and bitterness in the church is being revealed, and much of it is not righteous indignation: it's destructive. As I observe and listen to people's conversations concerning the source of their anger, what they describe can first appear acceptable and biblical—issues like church hurt, justice, passion, discernment, and even matters of truth—but in many cases, they are far from those things. When our anger becomes uncontrollable, defamatory, divisive, and destructive, have we not become pawns in the hands of an ancient foe?

Some people are angry with God, and some are angry with people who are associated with God but, ironically, only love those who support their personal causes. However, Matthew 5:22 says, "But I say to you that whoever is angry with his brother without a cause shall be in danger of the judgment" (NKJV). This is a fascinating verse. The phrase "without a cause" is not in the original Greek manuscripts. It's only written in the King James Version and The New King James Version. Most modern translations omit it. According to most scholars, there are several reasons why it was added, but that is not my concern in this setting. Instead, I intend to help the hearer understand the context of what Christ is saying, so they can make the proper adjustments and live accordingly.

There is clearly an anger that's acceptable and an anger that is not (Eph. 4:26). A healthy anger produced by the Holy Spirit is called "righteous anger." It's anger under control and not reckless in behavior or speech. It's anger that is not vindictive or pugnacious. It's anger that is grieved because God is grieved. It's anger that's been provoked by evil because that evil has perverted God's internal attributes and his word. It's anger rooted in God's holiness and governed by his mercy. It's God-centered and not driven by man. Matthew 5:22 does not speak of righteous anger but rather about sinful anger that rests in the bosom of carnal and foolish men (Eccles. 7:9).

The anger that Jesus is referring to is called *orgizo*. It's an anger that resides within individuals who don't follow the leading of the Holy Spirit consistently or have spiritual wounds they have not submitted to the Holy Spirit to be completely healed; therefore, they succumb to satanic plans and activities. It's a simmering, festering anger that conceals itself under the surface and refuses to be quenched. It is impulsive and explosive at any given moment if something is not to its liking. Think of the selfishness of the prophet Jonah (Jon. 4:9–11). He was so blinded by his anger that he was unwilling to participate with God in showing mercy to people headed toward eternal misery. It's a deep-seated rage and bitterness that is spiteful, condescending, and unforgiving. It refuses to let go of past grievances and looks for ways to retaliate, blame, and accuse. It's an anger that will overlook a God-sent deliverance moment in the present just to continue to focus on what caused that anger. It's an easily provoked anger that produces strife, gossip, rivalries, slander, tantrums, and jealousy. Proverbs 10:18 tells us, "Whoever hides hatred has lying lips, And whoever spreads slander is a fool" (NKJV). Hatred that's deceitful or dishonest creates an attitude of self-righteousness and victimization where everyone is wrong except the one who is angered.

Think of Cain (Gen. 4:1–15). Cain was so angered by what he perceived as unfairness on God's part that he refused to respond to God's call for mercy. Therefore, he murdered his brother Abel without any conviction of his sin. When someone feels they have been mistreated by God, it's not hard for them to carry out mistreatment on others. Scripture tells us to "Make no friendship with an angry man, and with a furious man do not go, lest you learn his ways and set a snare for your soul" (Prov. 22:24–25 NKJV). A moment of anger can cause you an eternity of emotional emptiness. Think of the older brother in the parable of the lost son taught by Christ (Luke 15:11–32). He was so driven by his point of view and anger that even his father's pleading could not reroute his emotions. Therefore, anger caused him to stand outside the door while inside, humility celebrated.

Let us not be deceived; our human anger cannot bring forth God's purpose, plan, or righteousness (James 1:19–20). When Satan sees such a mindset and climate of hostility, he will blend in and make himself at home. He will create an unstable, restless, and combative environment in the thoughts of the people in that particular location. Paul warns us in Ephesians to handle anger correctly because if we don't, we lend room to satanic control (Eph. 4:26–27). When we are angry, and our emotions are in overdrive, the last thing we want to do is hear, discern, and submit to the voice of God—and this is exactly what Satan wants.

Sadly, the fallout of the pandemic has brought an end to many godly relationships because hostility does not desire to surrender to God's ways and word. Therefore, people resort to states of abandonment, isolation, and resentment. In fact, Proverbs 18:1 states, "A man who isolates himself seeks his own desire; He rages against all wise judgment" (NKJV).

> *There are only three outcomes in a spiritual battle: you can become a prisoner of war, a casualty of war (from enemies or friendly fire), or a victor in war. When you are a prisoner, Satan takes you captive and makes you his spoil. He convinces you that you are doing the work of God while you are really working for Satan (2 Tim. 2:24–26). If you lack spiritual preparation and are not wearing your shield of faith, Satan can target you, hit you, and dismantle your faith with his darts. And Satan will shoot strategic darts when he knows your trust in God is suspect. He doesn't waste his arrows.*
>
> *You can become a casualty of war because of friendly fire. My oldest brother has a purple heart from his service in the Persian Gulf War—he was a casualty of war. But he was not hit by the enemy. Another US gunman mistook him and other soldiers as the enemy and hit their tank. My brother didn't die, but he experienced health challenges resulting from the friendly fire. What a great tragedy but a triumph for the enemy when God's people lack spiritual awareness and wound their own.*

Hostility's Roots Revealed

The pandemic did not create hostility. It revealed hostility and several things that previously only God had seen.

First, the pandemic revealed that coming to church pre-COVID was a formality for some people, not a necessity.

It wasn't a desire for them like it was for David, who said in Psalm 122:1, "I was glad when they said to me, 'Let us go into the house of the LORD'" (NKJV). Unfortunately, the outcome of the pandemic has convinced many to believe church attendance is not essential. When the physical doors of the church closed for a time, they became convinced they don't need the local church. In essence, we are seeing a deceitful spirit at work in their lives (Heb. 10:25). When you are in fellowship with the world, you look forward to participating in the things of the world. But when you are born again, your spirit longs to be among other like-minded believers.

Nonetheless, the local church is not an unblemished place. It's constantly under attack by Satan to undermine and hinder its mission and purpose (Rev. 2:8–10). The day you join, you add your flaws, personal preferences, past experiences and opinions to a community already treading water. An approved and appointed church is not without marks. Still, it should show evidence of a pattern of sound doctrine (orthodoxy) that shapes and fashions right behavior (orthopraxy), be submitted to the leading and work of the Holy Spirit, demonstrate God's will in and through growing disciples, and be striving toward spiritual maturity that produces Christ-like fruit (Phil. 3:12–15).

Because the church is not a flawless gathering, it is a great place to perfect one's love. Love is not perfected in circumstances we control; it is developed in the midst of the unexpected. We do not earn any kudos from the Lord by loving those who love us back (Luke 6:32). The true test is in loving those who are less than desirable in their actions. Love is not necessarily a work; it's a fruit of the Spirit (Gal. 5:22). You can do great works of humanitarianism and still not be motivated by love (1 Cor. 13:3). A work produces something, but fruit is always grown out of something. Jesus knows how to tailor-make circumstances to challenge and develop your love. Usually, these circumstances and environments are not ideal or desirable, but they are purposeful for your maturity.

There is a reason Christ teaches throughout the gospels about loving one another. Why? Because the church is a place where people who would have been adversaries in the world must now become people willing to lay down their lives for one another (John 15:13). If you only care for those who care for you, Jesus said you are no different from sinners, which means your love has not been developed (Matt. 5:46).

Many erroneously believe *they* are the church, and therefore gathering together is optional. Well, that's incorrect. The Greek word for church is *ekklesia*. It means the assembly or gathering of those who have been called out to a public place for the purpose of deliberating. Truth be told, there are some blessings that God will only unfold as we gather among the redeemed (Ps.133:1–3). God is in the gathering business, not isolation.

Second, the pandemic revealed that Christ's lordship was not a genuine desire for most.

Many were coming to church, saying that Jesus was their Savior, but they failed to acknowledge his lordship. Saving is what he does, but Lord is who he is. His scars are for what we have done, but his crown is for who he has always been. As Savior, he brought us out of sin. As Lord, he walks us into glory. Many appreciate him as the Savior but don't live like he is King. We have domesticated the Lion of Judah and have turned him into a personal kitten.

In the New Testament, Christ is referred to as *Lord* more often than any other title. In the book of Acts alone, he is mentioned as Lord over eighty times and called Savior only twice. He is Lord and Savior. He rules with absolute authority. Therefore, he demands absolute submission. He is not subservient to the whims and wishes of men: he is Lord. A king does not exist to serve the will of the people; the people exist to serve the will of the king. God's kingdom begins in us through the lordship of Christ, and his kingdom manifests among us in our discipleship. He looks for those who desire to become his full-time possessions, not for those who serve him only to be enriched by earthly possessions (1 Tim.

6:3–6). He will never approve or trust a man who cannot surrender to his command.

It's hard to believe that from March to December 2020—all those months of being out of the church (a local, physical gathering), with some out even longer due to particular dynamics—some believers have been led astray to their current state and spirituality. This outcome reveals there was a problem before the pandemic. If you were part of this number, I encourage you to ask yourself what or who has changed you to the point that you are confused about what is true? What has created such internal disturbance that you find it hard to find the true peace of God? What has convinced you to abandon and even demonize the very thing you once celebrated and found life in? There used to be an excitement in you to be in the house of the Lord, so much that you actively recruited others to join you. In the words of Paul to the church in Galatia, "You ran well. Who hindered you from obeying the truth" (Gal. 5:7 NKJV)?

We have to be able to discern God's voice, especially when Satan is crafting for us what I call the "*me* moment." What is a me moment? It's a moment when you numb yourself to God's instructions and warnings because you're blinded by your own narratives and passions. While you are convinced you are living your best life, a satisfying life, a "peaceful" life, you really have no idea that the worst moment of your life is on the horizon. There is no greater danger than a heart at peace, relaxed, and at ease while you're living in rebellion (Jonah 1:4–6).

Think of the people living in the city of Sodom just days and hours before judgment was revealed from heaven. They were functioning during a time marked by overwhelming spiritual delusion with a business-as-usual attitude. Yet they were moments away from a crisis that would determine their eternal existence. They were building, planting, selling, and buying, with no concern for others. In the pursuit of happiness, they were living by their own standards, living life to the fullest, until suddenly, the life they celebrated under false pretenses came to an unexpected ending. Sadly, there was no remedy (Luke 17:26–30).

Third, the pandemic has revealed that in their hearts, people believe patriotism equals Christianity, and that if you are not a "great patriot," you somehow cannot be a great Christian.

Do you know how many believers are no longer friends because they disagree with one another over who got elected? We've allowed the politics of an election to ruin heavenly friendships. May we be constantly reminded that this world is not our home and that our citizenship is in heaven (Phil. 3:20). This type of patriotism merged with religious belief is dangerous, and it's called Christian nationalism. It's neither scriptural nor is it of Christ.

We must be careful because it can produce mindsets similar to those during the Nazi regime. In his rise to power, Adolf Hitler placed the churches in Germany in a spiritual coma under the mantra of nationalism, and then he carried out his diabolical scheme. You can be so proud to be an American that you find yourself in the eternal fires of hell. And no, I'm not knocking what God has allowed us to have in this nation. But we can't get so puffed up that we think being American and "defending" our country makes us righteous. Mark this down: When the church marries politics, the spirit of politics will turn her from a glorious bride into a shameful harlot.

There is a difference between patriotism and nationalism. Patriotism is concern for one's country that allows one, without personal bias, to critically diagnose the good and the bad. Nationalism, in contrast, is idolatry of a country that causes one to have an elitist, slanted and misleading view. When a culture has been influenced to ignore facts, to defend blatant lies, to jeer at disabilities, and to gloat at other people's demise, the destructive sin of nationalism has progressed. And what makes this sin especially egregious is when so-called Christians use the name of Christ to promote works that lead to the instability and fragmentation of a country—like rioters carrying the Christian flag while stampeding across the floor of the House of Representatives.

Last, the pandemic revealed inner, private issues many already had with God.

The lockdown period openly revealed what God had always seen in the heart. This pandemic has allowed hidden spiritual cancers to be exposed. What if you already had an internal issue with God, the pandemic happened, and your loved one contracted the virus and passed away? Or you suddenly lost your income? What if you personally contracted the virus, and it seems you have still not fully recovered? What if you had some prolonged, hidden contention in your heart toward a brother or sister in the church, and when vitriol, hate, and division were played out before the entire world, and he or she didn't respond the way you expected or desired, it fueled your inner dislike for them?

When Satan knows the vulnerabilities in our hearts, he doesn't have to shoot too many arrows before he gets us. How can you detect that a deadly spiritual poison has spread within you? How can you tell if you have become a casualty of Satan's arrows? One telling detail is if your life has become consumed by self-centered, self-focused living. You no longer desire to seek and live out the will of God. Instead, you are driven to do what you think is right for yourself, regardless of what others think. You have begun to live a self-governed life while convincing yourself you are still serving Christ. In this condition, you run the danger of believing that the only people speaking the truth are those who agree with you.

How many times have we missed being strengthened or encouraged by God because, in our hour of difficulty, we wanted whoever God was using at that moment to acknowledge and agree with our perception?

God's witnesses do not come to affirm our feelings but to shift our attention to God's perspective. How often have we walked away discouraged when God desired to uplift us? It's called self-deception. Satan is called the great deceiver because of his ability to mirror the authentic works of God. Satan's objective is to take something artificial and make it look genuine, to take something synthetic and make it look authentic. He camouflages unlawful behavior to make it look like obedience. He imitates autonomy to make it look like righteousness. He disguises disobedience to make it look like biblical freedom. He makes his rewards look like God's blessings. He makes presumption look like biblical faith. He takes coincidence and makes it look like God's providence. He disguises pride to look like courage. It's a life of spiritual independence that has created a false boldness among believers; therefore, in this false sense of emotions, we misdiagnose the people who were placed in our lives by God. We see such behavior played out between Ahab and Micaiah. Second Chronicles 18:14–17 says,

> Then he came to the king; and the king said to him, "Micaiah, shall we go to war against Ramoth-Gilead, or shall I refrain?"
>
> And he said, "Go and prosper, and they shall be delivered into your hand!"
>
> So the king said to him, "How many times shall I make you swear that you tell me nothing but the truth in the name of the Lord?"
>
> Then he said, "I saw all Israel scattered on the mountains, as sheep that have no shepherd. And the Lord said, 'These have no master. Let each return to his house in peace.'"

> And the king of Israel said to Jehoshaphat, "Did I not tell you he would not prophesy good concerning me, but evil?" (NKJV)

See, Ahab was convinced Micaiah was his enemy because he was not cosigning on his "happiness." But Ahab had a history of not liking people who disagreed with what made him happy. So what was the end result? A great division marked by deep hostility. We saw the same outcome during the pandemic. Indeed, it's sad that all it took was a pandemic to reveal what has been brewing in people's hearts.

When we start talking about the eight characters in Second Chronicles, we are not concerned about gender. We are concerned with mannerisms and character traits. What you find at the foundation of hostility is people divided because of enmity due to seeing something two different ways. Ahab knew better but did what he wanted due to his humanistic view—a belief that promotes self-love and self-happiness over everything else. It's what gives idolatry life.

Think about this: Adam and Eve became the first casualties of spiritual warfare. In spiritual warfare, Satan opposes a godly perspective to get you to see things his way. Satan moved Adam and Eve from a theocentric view to a humanistic one (Gen 3:6). The shocking thing is that this happened while they were in the will of God. Yet as they turned and God was no longer at the center of their lives, self became the focus. And when it's all about you, you become your own god and how you feel becomes your truth. Adam and Eve had the freedom to eat from all the trees in the Garden of Eden except one (Gen. 2:16–17), and they were content—at least, that is, until Satan appeared and highlighted what was off-limits. In Ahab's case, he was upset because Micaiah's prophecy restricted his freedom. This scheme still happens today, where any limitation for our good is automatically deemed legalism.

When you know everything is created for God's glory, you have contentment with what God has allowed you to partake in. But to create opposition, Satan will try to convince you that what you can't partake in is a legalistic restriction and that God is trying to hold out on goodness for you. Adam and Eve enjoyed undisturbed peace and joy when they realized the Garden of Eden was for the will and the pleasure of God, but temptation became irresistible when Satan convinced them that the garden was really for their desires, their freedom, and their pleasures.

The emerging belief system rising out of the body of Christ since the pandemic is a synthetic Christian view. It is humanism laced with scripture and biblical terminology. It's syncretism, where that which is true and biblical loses its potency because it is paired with something diametrically opposed to it. When syncretism makes its way into the church, philosophical reasoning and new-age terminology mingle with Christian language and practices, and they are perceived as new and relevant. At the core of it all is Satan, repackaging humanism to a generation conditioned to pursue the love of self.

Humanism is a system of thoughts that centers on personal values, capacities, and worth. One's worth comes through their reasoning. True biblical Christianity says the end of all things in one's life is the glory of God. But with humanism, the end of all things is one's own happiness. The pandemic has produced a church culture in which the aim is to be happy and that therefore determines its choices at the expense of God's will. This compromised church culture believes if a decision does not bring personal enjoyment, then it cannot be the plan of God.

Second Chronicles 18 is a sad and similar story. It cautions us of the dangers of excluding God from our plans, thinking the ending will be blissful. What makes the story even more alarming is that with all the warning signs that were present, it should never have ended the way it did.

Chapter 5

The Demise of Ahab

Unjust anger should never rest in the bosom of a believer because it attracts satanic manifestations. Paul says, "Be angry and sin not," because if we allow anger to turn to sin, we give room to Satan (Eph. 4:26–27). By not controlling or correctly processing our anger, we open the door to oppression in our minds, yield ground and pass control over our lives to Satan. Anything we allow Satan to use yields unfavorable end results. Satan can make the beginning of any situation look sweet to rock us asleep. I'm not talking about beginnings, though, because the scriptures reveal that while there will be a way that seems right, its end will be destructive (Prov. 14:12). You won't find a favorable end anywhere in the Bible for those whom Satan has influenced.

If God did not have an issue with Ahab, then Ahab wouldn't have had a problem with the prophet Micaiah. Sometimes we have an issue with certain truths on earth because there is a possibility God has an issue with us in heaven. This is what Jesus was saying in the Gospel of John chapter 8:

"I know that you are Abraham's descendants, but you seek to kill me because my word has no place in you. I speak what I have seen with My Father, and you do what you have seen with your father."

They answered and said to Him," Abraham is our father."

Jesus said to them, "If you were Abraham's children, you would do the works of Abraham. But now you seek to kill Me, a Man who has told you the truth which I heard from God. Abraham did not do this. You do the deeds of your father."

Then they said to Him, "We were not born of fornication; we have one Father—God."

Jesus said to them, "If God were your Father, you would love Me, for I proceeded forth and came from God; nor have I come of Myself, but He sent Me. Why do you not understand My speech? Because you are not able to listen to My word. You are of *your* father the devil, and the desires of your father you want to do. He was a murderer from the beginning, and does not stand in the truth, because there is no truth in him. When he speaks a lie, he speaks from his own *resources*, for he is a liar and the father of it. But because I tell the truth, you do not believe Me. Which of you convicts Me of sin? And if I tell the truth, why do you not believe Me? He who is of God hears God's words; therefore you do not hear, because you are not of God." (Vv. 37–47 NKJV)

Let's look at verse 48. It says, "Then the Jews answered and said to Him, 'Do we not say rightly that You are a Samaritan and have a demon?'" When people are under a lying spirit, they start making up stuff, hoping something will stick. They call Jesus a demon, yet they feel like they know God.

Consider verses 49–59:

> Jesus answered, "I do not have a demon; but I honor My Father, and you dishonor Me. And I do not seek My *own* glory; there is One who seeks and judges. Most assuredly, I say to you, if anyone keeps My word he shall never see death."
>
> Then the Jews said to Him, "Now we know that You have a demon! Abraham is dead, and the prophets; and You say, 'If anyone keeps My word he shall never taste death.' Are You greater than our father Abraham, who is dead? And the prophets are dead. Who do You make Yourself out to be?"
>
> Jesus answered, "If I honor Myself, My honor is nothing. It is My Father who honors Me, of whom you say that He is your God. Yet you have not known Him, but I know Him. And if I say, 'I do not know Him,' I shall be a liar like you; but I do know Him and keep His word. Your father Abraham rejoiced to see My day, and he saw *it* and was glad."
>
> Then the Jews said to Him, "You are not yet fifty years old, and have You seen Abraham?"
>
> Jesus said to them, "Most assuredly, I say to you, before Abraham was, I AM."
>
> Then they took up stones to throw at Him; but Jesus hid Himself and went out of the temple, going through the midst of them, and so passed by. (NKJV)

Jesus said they could not hear him because they didn't know God. Our reaction to earthly conflict can be a good indicator of whom we belong to. If we cannot distinguish between the prophets who are true and those who are false, there is a great chance that we will be unable to distinguish between the God who is true and Satan who works hard to appear to be like God. A wrong perception of who God is will create a false assumption of where we stand with him.

If Ahab had been in harmony with God, then Micaiah's voice would have been favorable to him. Usually when we hear about Ahab, we hear about who he married—Jezebel (1 Kings 16:31). This decision marked the beginning of his downfall because he married somebody who did not value God's standards. Let's dig deeper into Ahab's background.

Ahab was one of 19 kings from the northern kingdom, and not one king in the north was righteous. Not one. Jeroboam, the first king in the north, set a negative standard, and the other kings followed suit (1 Kings 14:16). Ahab was the eighth king in this succession. Remember, as I mentioned earlier, each king had a prophet assigned to them. For example, for every King Saul, there was a Samuel (1 Sam. 15:1–35); for every King Jeroboam, there was the young prophet and Ahijah (1 Kings 13:1–13; 14:1–18); for every King Jehoiakim there was a Jeremiah (Jer. 26:1–24). And even for the nation of Israel, there was a John the Baptist (Luke 3:1–20).

So we can see how God regards Ahab based on his assigned prophet. Ahab was so addicted to evil and therefore so brazened in his heart concerning gross wickedness that God had to raise up a prophet just as emboldened as Ahab, but in the way of God's heart. Who did God give Ahab? Elijah. His name in Hebrew means, "My God is Yahweh." Elijah was rugged, a spartan, and had a no-nonsense personality. His name alone tells us a lot about what God thought about Ahab's worship. It reveals, by contrast, the severity of Ahab's beliefs—or lack thereof—that God had to provide someone like Elijah to confront him.

Consider 1 Kings 16. Verses 29–33 say,

> In the thirty-eighth year of Asa king of Judah, Ahab the son of Omri became king over Israel; and Ahab the son of Omri reigned over Israel in Samaria twenty-two years. Now Ahab the son of Omri did evil in the sight of the LORD, more than all who were before him. And it came to pass, as though it had been a trivial thing for him to walk in the sins of Jeroboam the son of Nebat, that he took as wife Jezebel the daughter of Ethbaal, king of the Sidonians; and he went and served Baal and worshiped him. Then he set up an altar for Baal in the temple of Baal, which he had built in Samaria. And Ahab made a wooden image. Ahab did more to provoke the LORD God of Israel to anger than all the kings of Israel who were before him. (NKJV)

Keep in mind that he's already wicked—more wicked than the other kings who lived before him. To add insult to injury, he marries a pagan worshiper, Jezebel. He consistently provoked God with his choices because he did not want to obey. First Kings 18:15–18 says,

> Then Elijah said, "As the LORD of hosts lives, before whom I stand, I will surely present myself to him today."
>
> So Obadiah went to meet Ahab, and told him; and Ahab went to meet Elijah.
>
> Then it happened, when Ahab saw Elijah, that Ahab said to him, "Is that you, O troubler of Israel?"
>
> And he answered, "I have not troubled Israel, but you and your father's house have, in that you have for-

saken the commandments of the LORD and have followed the Baals." (NKJV)

Ahab called Elijah the "troubler of Israel," but Elijah was not the one disobeying God. Ahab always had an issue with prophets and the truth. It was his personality. His appetite for perversion and his warped belief system created the hostility. Two diametrically opposed belief systems clash in these characters: one is theocentric (Elijah), and the other is humanistic. Ahab has a position as a king, but his view is humanistic. So many people are not theocentric at heart; they want to be self-governed. We have seen the evidence throughout the pandemic.

A theocentric mindset means one understands God is the author; therefore, he writes the story. But a humanistic mindset says we are the authors, and God is simply a reference we use to help us write our own stories. Keep in mind idols create idolatry. Idolatry stems from a religious system of beliefs that breeds humanism. It looks to substitute and supplant the truth, the reality, and the requirement of God into something that caters to one's preferences.

In a theocentric life, one lives and makes adjustments in a way that puts God at the center and makes him the main focus. When we have a theocentric worldview, we realize that everything flows from God and is generated by him. This worldview creates a biblical mindset in which our thoughts and minds are recalibrated to the word of God, which becomes the lens through which we filter our lives (Rom. 12:1–2).

Our minds are not inclined to think in a theocentric manner. It's much easier for us to think carnally because our flesh prefers it. But please, understand this: how we process thoughts can put us in bad standing with God. A thought life dishonorable to God eventually leads to a mindset that attracts demonic influence. And when demons influence the mind, it leads to a neglect of God's known will in favor of the individual's will (1 Chron. 21:1–4). God's will and way come to be viewed as optional, while personal choices become the priority. There can't be a biblical renewal of our minds unless we first submit ourselves to God. There is a difference between knowing scripture and being renewed by it. A renewed mind produces a recalibration to biblical thinking, which therefore produces right living (Eph. 4:20–24).

Scripture never supports human autonomy. Ahab believed God should sign off on his personal desires. This is why Ahab had an issue with anyone who came against what he wanted. When our thoughts become humanistic, another spirit is working to mislead us, and it's not the Holy Spirit. The Holy Spirit will never influence us to live independently of God.

***

A post-truth climate can only be achieved in an environment where truth was once believed. What is the meaning of *post-truth*? In 2016, Oxford University Press selected *post-truth* as its international word of the year. Living in a post-truth age means we live in a time when truth and facts are obsolete. This mode of thought holds that objective facts are less important than one's opinions, beliefs, or feelings. It's an age where perceptions triumph over reality and lies are repeatedly spoken without visible consequences. It's an age in which dishonesty is considered harmless, especially if it helps to fulfill one's own objectives.

Simply put, the post-truth age is an age of glorified falsehoods. You can't say *post-truth* in a place where truth was never valued. When we are exposed to God's truth, we become a target for Satan's lies since he takes satisfaction in moving us away from the truth. So, ironically, one of the greatest dangers to our walk with God is being exposed to the truth. If Adam and Eve had not previously been obedient to a truth Satan knew, there would have been no need for Satan to show up.

When the end goal becomes being happy by whatever means necessary, we become sensitive to and disorderly toward anyone who disagrees with us. Ahab exhibited this tendency throughout his life. We see it when he calls Elijah a troubler of Israel. In appealing to emotionally charged feelings over truth, he shows his deep desire to be accepted on his own terms. When someone doesn't want to live by the truth, they will try to appeal their way into the heart of people to get what they want. To gain their hearts, they will manipulate others' emotions. This action reflects the classic mindset of an opportunist—rather than being guided by consistent principles or plans, an opportunist exploits circumstances to gain an immediate advantage. When an opportunist sees a chance to gain an advantage from a situation, they will jump at it, frequently at the expense of ethics or morals.

***

Ahab had built a palace in Samaria, which was next to Jezreel. Joshua had given each tribe their inheritance, and, interestingly, Issachar was given the land in Jezreel (Josh. 19:17–23). The tribe of Issachar was prophetic; they knew the times and seasons of what Israel should do (1 Chron. 12:32). Something interesting happens when Ahab enters into a covenant with Jezebel. When he marries her, she builds her place in Jezreel. The story illustrates how Satan strategically defiles anything prophetic. If the prophetic voice became perverted or void, the people of God would have been at a disadvantage in warfare and in heeding God's urgent instructions (1 Sam. 3:1; Prov. 29:19). Trust me, Satan values and takes particular interest in things we are suspicious of or think are not that important. He believes more than we do: this is why he hits us with unbelief.

Beginning at 1 Kings 21:2, we read:

> So Ahab spoke to Naboth, saying, "Give me your vineyard, that I may have it for a vegetable garden, because it is near, next to my house; and for it I will give you a vineyard better than it. Or, if it seems good to you, I will give you its worth in money."
>
> But Naboth said to Ahab, "The LORD forbid that I should give the inheritance of my fathers to you!" (Vv. 2–3 NKJV)

The book of Numbers says the people were advised not to sell their land (36:7). Naboth, with a theocentric perspective, reflects that belief. But of course, Ahab does not care because he is humanistic. Naboth understood that he could not sell something given to him by God.

> So Ahab went into his house sullen and displeased because of the word which Naboth the Jezreelite had spoken to him; for he had said, "I will not give you the inheritance of my fathers." And he lay down on his bed, and turned away his face, and would eat no food. (1 Kings 21:4)

Ahab does not submit himself to the truth, and his negative emotional reaction is clear. He is a king, but his behavior is like a child's. He gets Jezebel to empathize with him and do what he knows is forbidden by God. He knows that it's unlawful, so he uses false emotions to get what he wants.

> But Jezebel his wife came to him and said to him, "How is it that your spirit is so sullen that you are not eating food?" So he said to her, "Because I spoke to Naboth the Jezreelite and said to him, 'Give me your vineyard for money; or else, if it pleases you, I will

give you a vineyard in its place.' But he said, 'I will not give you my vineyard.'" Jezebel his wife said to him, "Do you now reign over Israel? Arise, eat bread, and let your heart be joyful; I will give you the vineyard of Naboth the Jezreelite."

So she wrote letters in Ahab's name and sealed them with his seal, and sent letters to the elders and to the nobles who were living with Naboth in his city. Now she wrote in the letters, saying, "Proclaim a fast and seat Naboth at the head of the people; and seat two worthless men before him, and let them testify against him, saying, 'You cursed God and the king.' Then take him out and stone him to death."

So the men of his city, the elders and the nobles who lived in his city, did as Jezebel had sent word to them, just as it was written in the letters which she had sent them. They proclaimed a fast and seated Naboth at the head of the people. Then the two worthless men came in and sat before him; and the worthless men testified against him, even against Naboth, before the people, saying, "Naboth cursed God and the king." So they took him outside the city and stoned him to death with stones. Then they sent word to Jezebel, saying, "Naboth has been stoned and is dead."

When Jezebel heard that Naboth had been stoned and was dead, Jezebel said to Ahab, "Arise, take possession of the vineyard of Naboth, the Jezreelite, which he refused to give you for money; for Naboth is not alive, but dead." When Ahab heard that Naboth was dead,

Ahab arose to go down to the vineyard of Naboth the Jezreelite, to take possession of it. (Vv. 5–16 NIV)

Naboth stood on the word, and Ahab had a problem with that. But God saw it all, which is why he sent Elijah:

> Then the word of the LORD came to Elijah the Tishbite, saying, "Arise, go down to meet Ahab king of Israel, who lives in Samaria. There he is, in the vineyard of Naboth, where he has gone down to take possession of it. You shall speak to him, saying, 'Thus says the LORD: "Have you murdered and also taken possession?"' And you shall speak to him, saying, 'Thus says the LORD: "In the place where dogs licked the blood of Naboth, dogs shall lick your blood, even yours."'"
>
> So Ahab said to Elijah, "Have you found me, O my enemy?"
>
> And he answered, "I have found you, because you have sold yourself to do evil in the sight of the LORD: 'Behold, I will bring calamity on you. I will take away your posterity, and will cut off from Ahab every male in Israel, both bond and free. I will make your house like the house of Jeroboam the son of Nebat, and like the house of Baasha the son of Ahijah, because of the provocation with which you have provoked Me to anger, and made Israel sin.' And concerning Jezebel the LORD also spoke, saying, 'The dogs shall eat Jezebel by the wall of Jezreel.' The dogs shall eat whoever belongs to Ahab and dies in the city, and the birds of the air shall eat whoever dies in the field."

> But there was no one like Ahab who sold himself to do wickedness in the sight of the LORD, because Jezebel his wife stirred him up. And he behaved very abominably in following idols, according to all that the Amorites had done, whom the LORD had cast out before the children of Israel.
>
> So it was, when Ahab heard those words, that he tore his clothes and put sackcloth on his body, and fasted and lay in sackcloth, and went about mourning.
>
> And the word of the LORD came to Elijah the Tishbite, saying, "See how Ahab has humbled himself before Me? Because he has humbled himself before Me, I will not bring the calamity in his days. In the days of his son I will bring the calamity on his house." (Vv. 17–29 NKJV)

Notice that in verses 27–29, Ahab showed signs of repentance by tearing his clothes, and God showed him mercy. At this specific moment, he benefits from prophecy, but later on, he becomes an enemy of true prophecy and abhors the very appearance of Micaiah. Ahab is a recipient of divine mercy but a failure in the application of mercy. He neglects the privileges that mercy has granted him; therefore, he positions himself to become adversarial against God. First Kings 22 says,

> Now three years passed without war between Syria and Israel. Then it came to pass, in the third year, that Jehoshaphat the king of Judah went down to visit the king of Israel.
>
> And the king of Israel said to his servants, "Do you know that Ramoth in Gilead is ours, but we hesitate

to take it out of the hand of the king of Syria?" So he said to Jehoshaphat, "Will you go with me to fight at Ramoth-Gilead?" (Vv. 1–3 NKJV)

This is significant because three years passed, and it seemed like nothing was happening. Not seeing immediate consequences can distort our view of where we stand with God. This is one of the pitfalls of deception. Solomon made a profound statement: "When a crime is not punished quickly, people feel like it's safe to do wrong" (Eccles. 8:11 NLT). But we should never interpret God's silence as evidence of an unlimited mercy that will refrain from executing judgment. When God is silent, he is either testing the righteous or is in observation mode to bring justice to the wicked. Three years later, God chose to remove Ahab.

Truth be told, Ahab does not hate Micaiah because he speaks false words. He knows Micaiah's words are true. He despises Micaiah because the prophet's words never confirm or affirm Ahab's desires (1 Kings 22:8). Ahab intentionally does not bring Micaiah to the table; if Jehoshaphat had never inquired, Micaiah would not have been on the scene. Ahab is such a master of deception that he intentionally concealed the truth, hoping that Jehoshaphat would believe what was false. Ahab launches a personal attack on Micaiah because he doesn't see that God has an issue with him. Sometimes people don't seek advice because they are not ready to be told they are wrong. Sometimes people seek out your opinion after they have already made a decision to see if your reaction brings them confirmation. We would have to ask Ahab: If Micaiah is so false, why did you counsel Jehoshaphat to put his royal garments on while you remained discreet? (1 Kings 22:30).

Ahab was so image driven that he tried to appear to others as if he could hear from God, but he was under a lie. When a person is under a lying spirit, they never commit to what they believe; they keep jumping around. This is Ahab's personality, and it's at the root of this story.

Other people are drawn into the drama, but it's really God's personal appointment with Ahab.

Because we currently live in the days of the great falling away—a time when those who first adored truth will go and marry a lie—the spirit of truth will never gain the kind of attention that the spirit of error will draw. We are watching as Satan makes people's lives enjoyable in rebellion. I will repeat: Everything Satan influences and directs is earmarked by rebellion. So we have to ask ourselves: Which character am I? We would do well to remember that Jehoshaphat tried to play the middleman, and it almost cost him his life. And without Ahab and his poor choices, we wouldn't have learned what was happening in heaven.

The sad reality is that God was willing to forgive Ahab, but Ahab was not willing to change.

Chapter 6

When Loyalty Becomes Lethal

Ahab lived for himself. If anyone was against him, Ahab automatically took that person for his enemy. Those in harmony with a lying spirit exaggerate their spiritual discernment as if they were defenders of truth when really, they are intolerant of the truth. This is Ahab. But let's now take a look into the character of Jehoshaphat. He was a godly man who struggled to see his blind spots. Because of his blindness, he had a head-on collision with God.

In 2 Chronicles 17, we discover the beginnings of Jehoshaphat's reign. At the time, he focused on the people learning about God and obeying him. Because of Jehoshaphat's heart and obedience, the fear of the Lord fell on all the kingdoms that surrounded Judah, so they dared not wage war against God's people. What a profound testimony that anyone should take joy in. So one would wonder, how could a man like this find himself in a situation where he has aligned himself with a known enemy of God and end up in dire circumstances that could prematurely end his life? The problem with Jehoshaphat was compromise and double thinking. You can't claim you love God but then co-sign on a lie.

What is double thinking? It's not the same as being double-minded. Double thinking is even more destructive because, with it, people hold two contrary beliefs at the same time. Either through not noticing or denying the contradiction, they accept both. A man named Obadiah provides an example of double thinking, and we will look at him in detail. The scriptures declare that because Obadiah feared the Lord, he hid God's prophets from Ahab and Jezebel and provided bread and water for them. Yet he willingly worked for Ahab and carried out functions against God's character. His double thinking leads to a confrontation with Elijah, who challenges him to get his master. Obadiah obeys but shows great fear (1 Kings 18:7–15). In essence, this was also Jehoshaphat's struggle. Double thinking, and ungodly accommodations, nearly led to Jehoshaphat's premature death.

From a biblical point of view, unhealthy spiritual compromise comes from combining or uniting contradictory values, beliefs, and practices that provoke God's displeasure and disapproval. Because it weakens principles and standards, spiritual compromise reduces the quality and value of one's convictions, which causes conformity to a muddled measurement. If you accommodate and appease ungodly behavior, and you begin to live below standards you know to be true, you have surrendered to unhealthy compromise.

Many dangers are associated with this type of spiritual compromise, but two are deadly to our walk with Christ. First, unhealthy compromise can change our spiritual palate. If our palate can be changed, our spiritual appetite can be altered. When our appetite has been downgraded, not only will our biblical affections, discernment, and priorities become misaligned, but we will no longer have a desire for sound or wholesome teachings (2 Tim. 4:3–4). In this condition, we will look for teachings that accommodate our current spiritual condition.

This is the beginning of apostasy—when we first question and deny truth and subsequently remove ourselves from a position we originally occupied to join a lie.

Second, what makes spiritual compromise dangerous is its usually slow and subtle progression. A gradual drift can be more lethal and deceptive than a swift turn. Drifting implies flowing past the mark that God intended. It means passing by an intended destination, unnoticed, due to one's spiritual compass being redirected through carelessness. That carelessness comes about through being overly preoccupied with worldly things.

Drifting begins a downward spiral, for it's a catalyst to many other harmful things that can affect our spiritual health. If we do not reorient to God's direction immediately, the end will be devastating. For example, complacency, worldliness, indifference, a reversal of priorities, and tolerance are the results of drifting due to compromise. Many things are acceptable to today's believers that believers in earlier eras would have found appalling. In the hands of Satan, compromise is a strategic, potent tool for dismantling our fellowship with God.

Seven Factors in the Compromise of Jehoshaphat

Let's look at seven things that highlight Jehoshaphat's compromise.

According to 2 Chronicles 17:1, Jehoshaphat initially strengthened himself against Israel. Who was Israel? During King Solomon's reign over Israel, Solomon deliberately rebelled against God's warnings against pursuing foreign women who would turn his heart to worship false gods (1 Kings 11:1–13). Because of his sin, God divided the kingdom in two—the northern kingdom was called Israel and the southern, Judah. Solomon's son Rehoboam was king of Judah during the split (12:1–24), and Jeroboam, Solomon's servant, became the first king of the north after the split (11:26–35). All nineteen kings who ruled the north were wicked, while there were occasionally righteous kings in the south, such as Jehoshaphat, Hezekiah, and Josiah.

Jehoshaphat fortified himself against Israel because the northern kingdom had established a pattern of detestable acts and transgressed and repeatedly defied God's commandments (2 Kings 17:7–23). The northern kingdom was not only a threat to Judah politically and militarily but, most importantly, from a spiritual standpoint. So the million-dollar question is this: why would Jehoshaphat strengthen himself against Israel but then join himself to Ahab, the king of Israel (2 Chron. 18:1)? Jehoshaphat knew the danger of being connected to Israel. How could a man with a testimony of having walked in the ways of the beloved King David fall this far (2 Chron. 17:3–6)? It's simple: he was ensnared by the deadly trap of spiritual compromise.

Jehoshaphat's first downfall was desiring acceptance from someone who did not share his view of God.

Is it wise to enter covenant relationships (business, marriage, etc.) with someone who doesn't share your view of God (2 Cor. 6:14–16)? To begin to answer this question, consider the following differences between Daniel and Obadiah. Obadiah first fed God's prophets but then turned and, by choice, worked for Ahab (1 Kings 18:1–16). In contrast, while Daniel also worked for a wicked king, he was taken by force to another land (Dan. 1:1–6). Out of convenience and fear, Obadiah served Ahab. While the nation suffered from drought, instead of finding food for humans, Obadiah searched the land to find food for Ahab's livestock.

The danger Jehoshaphat illustrates is that in joining with someone who doesn't have the same views, at some point, for the sake of loyalty, you will likely forsake the truth you know to keep your covenant. God was with Jehoshaphat, yet Jehoshaphat was willing to trade his eternal value for earthly acceptance. We should consider ourselves warned:

whatever we trade God in for will eventually make a greater demand out of us (2 Chron. 18:2–3).

In Jehoshaphat's time, marriage was used as a political strategy. If one nation or kingdom wanted to establish solidarity with another, strategically arranged marriages of key people from each kingdom could be used to encourage peace. Kings were responsible for arranging these marriages. This manipulative, political act shows the extreme depth that compromise for the sake of loyalty can take, for it hinders and distorts one's foresight. Jehoshaphat arranged for his son to marry the daughter of Ahab and Jezebel. Athaliah was not just an ungodly woman, she was sinister and diabolical. Jehoshaphat failed to see that she would eventually rise to seize the throne. She ruled Judah for seven years, and she sought to kill all descendants of the royal bloodline (2 Chron. 22:10–12).

Jehoshaphat's second downfall was his lack of trust in God.

Just in case God didn't come through for him, Jehoshaphat brokered a deal with an enemy of God. He was thinking, "What if God's favor and protection run out? Just in case, I'll mediate a deal where at least I can have peace with Israel." While peace may seem like an admirable, even godly goal, Jehoshaphat showed he did not trust God to achieve it. When we compromise for the sake of unity and peace, it may at first seem like a good thing. After all, there will be a season of temporary comfort. However, in the end, we will lose. When we sow to the flesh, we will not reap the good of the Spirit (Gal. 6:7–8). But God was already with Jehoshaphat, so why was he trying to make a deal?

There is a truth not discussed much in today's church: pragmatism has become the measuring tool for success and how pleased God is with us. We quantify our walk with God based on our financial freedom, possessions, and the personal liberty those material things feel like they grant us. When these perceived blessings become the benchmarks of discipleship, taking the broad path doesn't seem consequential (Matt. 7:13–14).

Yet Jesus sternly warned against the danger of covetousness. He instructed us that our lives do not consist of how many things we possess (Luke 12:15). What exactly is *covetousness*? It's a sin rooted in the love of self that causes an unhealthy desire for gain based on what others have. It causes competition for and pursuit of things off-limits or out of the will of God in order to gratify self. According to Paul, covetousness is idolatry (Col. 2:5). Idols are indeed present when one moves into covetous behavior.

An idol is any person, place, or thing from which I draw strength, comfort, peace, and security other than Christ—it brings contentment to the exclusion of the scriptures. When idols are served, a belief system called idolatry results. It can reflect any system of thought in which my personal beliefs replace God's truth, reality, and requirements. Idolatry results from humanity attempting to use a god to serve its self-conceived purpose. When you are subject to idolatry, you convince yourself that your idols are acceptable and not harmful to God. The idol positions itself as a god, while the true God makes concessions in the person's life concerning that specific idol. In essence, when people become covetous, their thoughts become their own counselor, which opens the door for idols to be freely and openly obeyed.

When an idol stands between a prophet and the people, the prophet will not be welcomed. A true prophet will never give allowances or modify God's message to be accepted by those with idols in their hearts. An idol in the heart is more lethal than a carved wooden statue. Covered with spiritual jargon to protect its identity, an idol can remain hidden (Ezek. 14:1–11).

Second Chronicles 18:1 provides a clue as to what led to Jehoshaphat's lack of trust and what can lead to ours. It says Jehoshaphat had riches and honor in abundance. Popularity, power, and riches can move one to a place where trust in God seems no longer necessary but has become optional. However, God repeatedly reminded the children of Israel about the danger of forgetting him because of their increase in riches (Deut. 6:10–12; 8:6–20). Money has the power to cause us to forget God—not intellectually, but spiritually. What does this forgetting look like? It looks like submission to God not being the same: we may become more independent in our decision-making because we've attained wealth; we may elevate protecting or gaining possessions above fully obeying God; we may take ownership of our wealth as if we were its source; we may develop an inverted view of the wealth in which we mislabel our greed and selfishness as "kingdom" investments. Materialism can be a terminal spiritual cancer in the life of a nation, a church, and an individual. It can cause us to become so indifferent that we completely misdiagnose our spiritual condition—just ask the church of Laodicea (Rev. 3:14–22).

When we have nothing or the bare minimum of what we need, we depend heavily on God. But when we accumulate resources, we often come up with "just-in-case" plans that we redefine as "wisdom." I'm not saying that having insurance or emergency funds shows a lack of faith. But as believers, we need to be careful not to allow increasing riches to impact our hearts to the point we no longer rely on God but instead on what we've accumulated. David tells us, "If your wealth increases, don't make it the center of your life" (Ps. 62:10 NLT). In no way am I implying that being wealthy is a sin. In his first letter to Timothy, Paul instructed him to command those rich in this present age (see 1 Tim. 6:17–19). If God is giving instructions to the rich, then that indicates that some, not all, in the body of Christ will be rich. So, being wealthy is not a sin, but being controlled or driven by wealth is. In the same verse in which Paul spoke about riches, he also warned not to exaggerate self-worth because of money and not to trust in it. Truth be told, comfort, accumulating possessions, or reaching a desired social status can make someone feel emboldened, important, and empowered in their decision-making. Ask Lot. He decided to dwell in the plain of the Jordan when he had generated possessions, not when he had nothing (Gen. 13:5–13). So, beware when a "better life" causes you to live independently of the will of God. Jehoshaphat, for example, was becoming one with someone on God's most wanted list.

We know how that ended.

In his third downfall, Jehoshaphat made a commitment based on appearances and convenience, not prayer.

Jehoshaphat's mistake reminds me of when Joshua and the Israelites made a covenant with the Gibeonites without consulting God (Josh. 9:1–16). After making the covenant, Joshua realized who the Gibeonites really were. He made a grave mistake that could not be altered. We make poor choices when we dedicate ourselves to things based on emotional connections and personal benefit. The commitment will be built upon a deck of cards, and collapse is inevitable.

Not every good situation we find is an answer from God. Biblical prayer does not change God; it changes us. It aligns and realigns us to the plan and purpose of God. But when someone has weakened themselves through compromise for the sake of loyalty to something other than God, praying for God to reveal his will is a façade. Truth be told, when one has been reduced to this spiritual state, anything in opposition to one's own ambitions will be overlooked, cast down, and downright rejected. A person in this position makes easy prey for seducing spirits, for coincidental circumstances will be mistaken for the providence of God.

Think about Jonah. In his compromised state, he found a boat leaving at the right time, and he had the right amount of money to ride the boat to take him to his desired destination (Jon. 1:1–3). If God, in his sovereignty, had not brought a storm, Jonah would have achieved his goal while living in rebellion. Because Christ warned us of lying spirits demonstrating false signs and wonders in the Last Days, I think it's important to stress this again. When we are out of rhythm with God, Satan will introduce coincidences that appear to be God's supernatural, providential work. This is Satan's agenda to move us onto a course foreign to heaven's agenda. It's an alternative course that looks ideal, seems logical, and feels appealing. When believers abandon the known will of God for their lives—this can apply to God's word or something specific God has revealed—Satan will always provide the financial means and create what seems to be a great opportunity to further their rebellion. But if we leave God out of the equation, we will eventually come to a regretful ending.

Cowardliness was Jehoshaphat's fourth downfall.

Jehoshaphat did not stand up for what he knew to be right. He knew something was not right because if he had believed the 400 prophets, he wouldn't have had to ask for someone else (2 Chron. 18:1–7). Ahab was under the control of a destructive spirit, and Jehoshaphat was influenced by that same spirit. When we are under the control of a lying spirit, confirmation becomes our source of truth. We come to believe only what we already believe—what validates our preconceived narrative. In the words of the late Danish theologian Søren Kierkegaard, "There are two ways to be fooled. One is to believe what isn't true; the other is to refuse to believe what is true."[1] When one is under the control of a deceiving spirit, one sees circumstances and views people the same way unscrupulous teachers view the scriptures: they twist the meaning of biblical words and put their desires at the center. They impose reasoning on the scriptures to support their own presuppositions.

---

[1] Søren Kierkegaard, *Works of Love: Some Christian Reflections in the Form of Discourses*, Howard Vincent Hong (translator). New York: Harper Perennial, 1964.

When we are being influenced, we have to be persuaded that the untruth is the truth, and the truth is a lie. Ahab is not encouraging Jehoshaphat to jump into God's business; he is trying to convince him to join a war to settle a personal desire. When you are under the control of a lie, Satan wants you to influence someone else (2 Tim. 3:13). Satan gets no joy from only deceiving one person. A lie has to convince others, which is why its beginnings must seem true and believable. This is why Solomon says there is a way that seems right to a man, but the end is destruction (Prov. 16:25). When we start to trust our wisdom, we move away from being Spirit led, for Solomon also warned us that "He who trusts in his own heart is a fool" (Prov. 28:26 NKJV).

It is worth noting here that Jehoshaphat stood by silently and watched Micaiah suffer verbal and physical mistreatment while knowing he was a true messenger of the Lord (1 Kings 22:8–27). Remaining mute while servants of God are mishandled and humiliated due to your misplaced loyalty is a travesty.

Jehoshaphat's fifth downfall was unbelief.

Jehoshaphat didn't believe God's prophet, the mouthpiece for God's counsel (2 Chron. 18:27). His willingness to continue in the same direction, even after asking for a word from God, shows how deeply he was entrenched in compromise. From a theological perspective, this gross spiritual negligence on Jehoshaphat's part could have led to his demise. While he initially rejected the counsel of 400 dishonorable prophets by asking for someone else, he ended up following the poor direction of that initial counsel after all. Insidious, inverted thinking like this happens when godly principles are subverted. Asking God for direction or an answer and not responding to his instructions is intentional deception. God's instructions are not designed to be attractive; they are spoken to be obeyed.

A similar behavior plays out against Jeremiah when the captains of the military and all the people ask for God's direction concerning their lives (Jer. 42:1–22). The people vow to obey the instructions of God, whether his answer pleases or displeases them. After ten days of seeking God, Jeremiah comes back with an answer, but when it's not what the people want to hear, they refuse the direction (43:1–13). According to Jeremiah, people who inquire of God with no intention of obeying his word are hypocrites in their hearts. They are spiritual pretenders—fraudsters. Pretending to desire his will in public but being determined to walk by your own counsel privately is a frightening game to play with God. Satan will convince you that you have gotten away with such a deplorable act and that consequences will be far and few, but it's only a matter of time because God will not be mocked.

Just ask Balaam (Num. 22:9–22).

Sixth, in Jehoshaphat's blindness, he allowed Ahab to dress him for a battle that had nothing to do with him.

In 2 Chronicles 18:29, we see the full effects of how far increasing compromise will bring you. It produces a blindness that results in what the Bible calls a stupor or stupidity (Rom. 11:8). (I will address this again later.) One has to wonder: If Ahab did not believe the word Micaiah spoke, then why did he disguise himself? Jehoshaphat submitted to the counsel of the ungodly by agreeing to Ahab's advice for him to put on his royal clothing. He went into a battle that was not his fight as the only clearly identifiable king. May we all learn a vital lesson from this: we should never put our confidence in a person who has become possessed by what this world values. Proverbs tells us, "Confidence in an unfaithful man in time of trouble is like a bad tooth and a foot out of joint" (25:19 NKJV).

Jehoshaphat was so deceived by his loyalty that he could not see that Ahab was setting him up to be killed. Ahab was like a wolf, self-focused and greedy. A wolf's very nature is predatory: you can't teach one how to care. Jehoshaphat sank so deeply into compromise that he could not discern that Ahab cared nothing about him. Mark this down: Personal desires unsubmitted to the will of God become an enemy to spiritual discernment. We need to be careful of people who teach and coach us on putting on garments God hasn't instructed us to wear and who lead us into assignments, ministries, and businesses heaven has not recognized. When King David was determined to go to war against Goliath, King Saul tried to offer him his armor and his sword; but as David put Saul's clothing on, he realized that he couldn't move for battle in them. As he removed the king's armor, he stated, "I cannot walk with these, for I have not tested them" (1 Sam. 17:39 NKJV). He then adorned himself with weapons that he had previously tested and had victory with—a sling and five stones.

When your spiritual life is on the line, and you find yourself against a problem that looks insurmountable, be wary of unproven, untested advice. Trust in what seems foolish; trust in what God taught you during your wilderness season. We serve a God who loves to take pleasure in things that seem weak and useless, things that seemingly have powerless beginnings (1 Sam. 17:45–50).

Finally, compromise moved Jehoshaphat to do something abominable and treasonous in the eyes of God: he strengthened the hands of someone wicked and loved someone who hated God.

Jehoshaphat's affinity for Ahab led to a severe rebuke from God. In our attempts to be loving and show our love, we must be careful who we align ourselves with. Not everyone who claims they love God love from his perspective and according to his standards (John 5:38–42). If you establish a covenant with those who have God on their lips but are enemies of Christ in their hearts, proving to them how loving you are can place you in precarious situations where your faith and your walk with God begin to hemorrhage (Ps. 50:16–23). In their presence, for example, you may find complaining, gossip, suspicion, unbelief, and faultfinding all defined as harmless venting. You know their speech and behavior are wrong, but you desire their friendship over telling them the truth. The late Adrian Rogers once said, "It's better to be divided by truth than to be united in error."[2] You know standing on the word of God will bring you into conflict with them, but because you know their temperament is hostile and explosive, you refrain and retreat. You want them to admire you, so you decide to just pray privately for them. We see this type of compromise during the days of Jeremiah when God was against the false prophets whose fraudulent messages were not convicting sinners but only strengthening their hands (Jer. 23:14).

God will always take issue with this sort of compromise. To be straightforward, it's not love: it's self-protective, cowardly behavior. It's image branding, not image crucifying. Yet God showed Jehoshaphat mercy and spared his life. Jehoshaphat had no clue how God saw Ahab; therefore, God raised a prophet to announce his displeasure with Jehoshaphat's decision to join God's enemy. The prophet posed a compelling, convicting diagnosis of how God saw the compromise. He asked Jehoshaphat, "Should you help the wicked and love those who hate the LORD? Therefore the wrath of the LORD is upon you" (2 Chron. 19:2 NKJV). Usually, if Satan has deceived you to become one with the very object about to be judged, you are supposed to receive the same judgment as the one who initiated it all. But God spared Jehoshaphat. However, the mercy of God should never be assumed; it's always extended by grace. Mercy could not be granted until Jehoshaphat first

---

[2] From a talk at the National Religious Broadcasters Convention, quoted in *The Berean Call*, "Quotable," December 1, 1996. https://www.thebereancall.org/content/december-1996-quotable.

knew how God felt about the situation. If God is going to extend mercy to you, you must first receive his correction. Mercy without knowing how God feels is unbiblical. Jehoshaphat was a great king, but his life was intermingled with a compromise that the Lord despised.

The Failure of Blind Loyalty

Jehoshaphat's errors show us that blind loyalty is not loyalty at all. It's self-serving, duplicitous, and deceptive, and it ultimately leads to a devastating corrosion of godly principles. If Satan can change your affections, then he can rearrange your appetite, and a change in appetite is an indicator that godly convictions are eroding. Likewise, a desire for comfort and unity can cause one to make ungodly accommodations and adjustments, all for the sake of avoiding conflict or contention. But a peace not guided by God's principles is a misleading peace. It will never bring true peace. In the end, it will only bring the loss of your voice. Jehoshaphat's willingness to join Ahab nearly cost him his life, producing irreversible consequences that would have been lived out for eternity.

So, in many circumstances, it truly is better to be divided by the truth than to be united by compromise.

Chapter 7

The Lying Spirit

In 2 Chronicles 18, the location, Ramoth-Gilead, is significant. God had determined to put an end to Ahab in Ramoth-Gilead (v. 19). Understanding this detail is important because God's will is often tethered to specific locations. The principle is displayed throughout scripture. For example, God told Abraham to leave his country and family and go to a place that he would show him (Gen. 12:1). God told Abraham to take his son, Isaac, and go offer him up as an offering on one of the mountains that he would show him (Gen. 22:2). Genesis 28 describes Jacob fleeing from his brother Esau, reaching a specific location, and falling asleep. He sees God standing above a ladder there, and God promises to bring Jacob back to that place. Jesus knew his death must take place at Jerusalem (Matt. 16:21). These are only a few examples of how locations are significant to God. Therefore, Satan's ultimate ambition is to move and keep you away from God's location to hinder you from fulfilling God's will. Satan will allow your life to prosper and be free from turmoil as long as you are not in the prescribed place.

Just as God's will is related to a location, so is his active judgment. God determined that Ramoth-Gilead would be where Ahab would fall. Ahab had been king for a while, and it seemed like he was getting away with his immoral behavior and idol worship. Ramoth-Gilead was a territory God gave to his people, the tribe of Gad, as part of their inheritance (Deut. 4:43). Moses had dispersed parts of the territories to different tribes (only the tribe of Levi didn't have an inheritance because God was their portion).

Ramoth-Gilead had been given to the people as a Levitical city of refuge (Josh. 21:38). Anyone who accidentally committed murder could go to the city and not be killed by those looking to avenge the murder. But the city known as a place of refuge was about to become a place where God would render his verdict against Ahab. Ramoth-Gilead was located forty miles east of Jerusalem, which means Jehoshaphat lived near the city. Now, because of Israel's unrepentant sin, God had allowed the Syrians to occupy Ramoth-Gilead. Ahab wanted to get something he felt belonged to him, so he persuaded Jehoshaphat to reclaim the area.

When the hand of God is against you, you can move to a place that you think will be better, but it will become a place of misery. Yet even in sin, Ahab believed he could achieve something great. Why? He believed a lie.

When you believe a lie, you have been persuaded. There is an important distinction between being controlled and being influenced by a lie: mercy is still available when you are influenced by a lie but it becomes limited when you are controlled by a lie. When you are controlled by a lie, Satan will use you to influence others and pass the lie on. Ahab was controlled by a lie, while Jehoshaphat was influenced by a lie. So, Jehoshaphat didn't die. He had mercy in his account because of his past obedience.

We need to inquire of God in everything we do because of our sin. When we make an unholy covenant, we allow our allegiance and loyalty to the covenant to override our obedience to God. Loyalty is a good trait unless it moves us to disobey God. The covenant Jehoshaphat cut with Ahab blinded him to God.

In some cases, when you begin to inquire of the Lord, the lie responds first. Satan will not get involved until you start to desire God. A lie will often run before the truth so that when the truth finally appears, it will seem like it's what's insane and will be hard to believe. But before we move further, I think it's important for us to define and understand the purpose of a lying spirit. Ignorance of the operation of this spirit will subject us to remaining spiritual infants in the hands of an ancient Deceiver.

The Lying Spirit Is the Essence of Satan

What is a lying spirit? It's a chief or ruling spirit that operates as an extension of Satan. As the Holy Spirit is to God, so is a lying spirit to Satan. It tries to imitate the workings of the Spirit among people in order to instruct, subvert, and divert. It can make circumstances and situations appear to be of God, to feel like God, and to sound like God. It works by convincing people that certain coincidental events are God's providential acts. This spirit is the very essence of Satan.

To encounter this spirit is to meet Satan himself. The Greek word for *lie* and *false* is *pseudo*. It indicates something that superficially appears to be or behaves like one thing but is really something else. It also means that which is coincidental, an imitation, and intentionally deceptive. It describes statements intended to deceive. Someone who tries to deceive knows a thing is not true but repeats the untruth to intentionally mislead. Lying spirits are experts in disseminating disingenuous information. Trying to overcome such attacks with human wisdom is a recipe for calamity. These same spirits enacted the deception which accelerated Jesus' death. Their influence and propaganda showed up in the mouths of the false witnesses to lend credibility to the agenda pushed by Jewish leaders.

You see, the Mosaic Law to which Jews ascribed had a system in place designed to provide legitimacy for finding a man guilty (Deut. 19:15–21). This is why when Jesus was on trial, at least two witnesses were required for him to be found guilty and be sentenced to death. Matthew 26 says,

> And the chief priests… and the whole Sanhedrin sought false witness against Jesus so that they might put him to death. And they found none, though many false witnesses came forward, they found none. But at the last two false witnesses came forward and said, He said, I am able to destroy the temple of God and in three days build it. (Vv. 59–61 DARBY)

In this kangaroo trial staged to find Christ guilty, the Sanhedrin leaders, in their vitriol against Christ, broke and violated the very rules they pretended to live by.

For example, according to their law, all evidence had to be guaranteed by two witnesses, who were separately examined and could not have contact with each other. A trial always began by bringing forth evidence for the innocence of the accused before evidence of guilt was offered. Any witness testimony proven false was punishable by death. In Jesus' case, there was no proof that the two witnesses had never spoken with each other. Also, there was no evidence in favor of Jesus presented first, nor was there any punishment for the many untrue testimonies.

On this note, there is a fundamental spiritual truth to understand: in their intense dislike for someone, people will go to extreme measures to disprove and undermine that person's character. Proverbs says, "An evildoer gives heed to false lips; A liar listens eagerly to a spiteful tongue" (17:4 NKJV). When a person has become a conduit for a lie and, therefore, tries to disqualify your image, they know they can't go at it alone—they will need a co-signer for their ungodly scheme. Finally, they found two individuals under the persuasion of a lying spirit to find Christ guilty. They had overheard Jesus say something about destroying the temple and raising it back up on the third day. They interpreted his statement to mean that Christ had a sinister plan concerning the temple, even though it was clearly evident that the temple Jesus spoke about was his body (John 2:19–21).

Understand this: False witnesses are skilled at taking bits and pieces of information to create false narratives to support their position. Under the influence of a lying spirit, such individuals will go to great lengths to twist, add, and subtract words and circumstances to push a demon-inspired agenda to destroy, injure, and cast suspicion upon those they see as an enemy or a threat (Prov. 25:18). At times, they provide partial truths for a relatively plausible argument, but the purpose of their testimony is to persuade listeners that their falsehoods are real. In God's kingdom, a half-truth is still a whole lie. A false witness always acts as an agent under Satan's control and is on his payroll. Everyone Satan has ever used eventually suffers a price for it.

The book of Proverbs is a collection of wise sayings and not necessarily of promises. But certain statements repeated often throughout the book imply eternal certainties. One repeated theme is the subject of a false witness. As a matter of fact, in chapter 19 alone, the Holy Spirit speaking through Solomon reveals a settled truth concerning such individuals. Verse 5 tells us this: "A false witness will not go unpunished, And he who speaks lies will not escape" (NKJV). Verse 9 ups the ante specifying that he "shall perish." Notice the assuredness of the word will—he *will* not go unpunished, *will* not escape God's all-knowing eye. Based on this projected outcome, it would be wise to let Satan know we are not available for his services.

In one of Christ's most combative and confrontational dialogues with Jewish leaders, he clearly identifies who Satan, the devil, really is (see John 8). To this point, it's important to understand that God changed Satan's name to make us aware of how Satan opposes us. His former name was *Lucifer*, meaning "light bearer," which describes his original purpose. However, because of his sin and subsequent removal from heaven, God changed his name to *Satan* and the *devil* to describe his current purpose (Luke 10:18) and to show and prepare us for our battle against him.

He is called *Satan* because he is our adversary and our opponent, who is continually hostile toward us. When he is being himself, his purpose is to resist us. In Revelation 12, he appears as an enormous red dragon with seven heads, ten horns, and seven crowns on its heads. The dragon represents persecution. When Satan pursues us with great persecution, it is to dissemble our trust and faith in Christ to cause us to renounce the gospel and give up on sacrificial living because the hardship and suffering are too costly. In the same chapter, he is called "the serpent of old," which recalls his plan of deception in the Garden of Eden. Notice that he did not show up in the garden as a dragon. He knew he could not persecute Adam and Eve because they were without sin. Instead, he got them through deception and slander, the same tools that had worked for him in heaven, which is how we come to understand his other name, the devil.

The Devil Is a Liar

The word *devil* is the translation of *diablos*, from which we get the English term "false accuser" or "slanderer." It means one who opposes the cause of God through lies and deceit. When Satan is the devil, his objective is to use slander. A slanderer utters false charges or misrepresentations designed to damage one's reputation. Satan wants us to be either victims or carriers of slander. When slander is the wile of his choice, he purposely causes you to hear lying and slandering statements to disengage your faith and stir up your anger. This is significant, and in John 8, Jesus makes a profound statement about it.

Discussing the issue of who the true seed of God is, Jesus hands over an indictment that boils the blood of his accusers. He tells them he knows their true father, and it's not Abraham, or his Father, God. He tells them their father is the devil, and their desires are just like their father's, the devil's (vv. 37–59). In his polemic argument, Jesus also provides an insight into the very nature of our adversary: "When he speaks a lie, he speaks from his own resources, for he is a liar and the father of it" (v. 44 NKJV). Notice his first words: "When he speaks a lie." Not *if* he speaks, but *when* he speaks. When he is the devil, he speaks; he talks; he repeats himself; he announces; he is heard. He does more damage by speaking than by physical affliction.

When the mind and thoughts are under attack through the constant bombardment of the devil's talk, it's spiritual warfare. The devil will repetitively speak to peoples' minds to persuade them to see circumstances from his perspective. We can sometimes see manifestations of this in a believer who has become overly discouraged, suicidal, depressed, and oppressed. While in these types of mental conditions, our enemy can cause us to lose hope through an avalanche of words. Jesus tells us that when the devil speaks, he can only speak one thing: a lie. He cannot speak the truth, and he can only speak lies because that's his very being. As God can only speak the truth because he is the essence and the source of truth, and his Spirit is true, the devil can only speak lies because he is the source of lying, and his spirit is a lie. Jesus tells us again that when the devil speaks, he speaks from his own nature and character. And what is his character? He is a liar.

It's one thing for humans to label one another as liars, but it's another thing for the Ancient of Days to call you one. Like a skilled prosecutor, Jesus ends his indictment with a startling truth about the devil: he is "the father of all lies." Contrary to popular opinion, while God is indeed over all things, he is not the *cause* of all things. God can use evil for good, but he is not the cause of evil. He can use a lie to accomplish a plan, but he is not the author of a lie. So when Jesus says that the devil is the father of all lies, it means that he is the source, the originator of deceit and deception. Satan's lies led to the first murder—the murder in the garden. He lied in heaven, and his tail drew one-third of the angels with him (Rev. 12:4), and his lies on earth will drag countless individuals into the lake of fire (Rev. 21:8).

Partial Truths and the Path Toward Progressive Deception

Let's look at Matthew 24 again because a lying or seducing spirit plays a vital role in how many will believe in someone who comes in Christ's name. Anytime you find deception and deviation, you will find a lying spirit in operation. The word *lie* is associated with deception because the objective of a lie is to deceive. "Jesus answered: 'Watch out that no one deceives you. For many will come in my name, claiming, "I am the Messiah," and will deceive many'" (Matt. 24:4–5 NIV). The purpose of deception is to get us to believe a false promise so that in the end, when the promise doesn't come to pass, we form a different opinion and view of God. Satan then will use this different view to distort the trustworthiness, believability, and faithfulness of God. Our faith primarily rests upon our perception of God's character, not necessarily his promises. Promises are more believable when we trust the character of those who speak them; hence, Satan seeks to misrepresent God's reliability. Who would lay down their life for a God they couldn't trust? This is the agenda of Satan, and the agents who help carry out this plan are false prophets. One reason why many will be deceived is that they will receive and believe spurious prophets who were not sent but simply went.

A false prophet is not only one who spoke something that did not come to pass; that's low-hanging fruit. When you begin to grow in your walk with the Lord, that level of deception is easy to spot. But as we get closer to Christ's return, there is a greater danger that is harder to discern. Satan gets cleverer. We will see more false signs and wonders manifested by lying spirits. They will produce what may seem to be miracles from God and will even receive affirmation for them (Deut. 13:1–18). But these prophets, under the influence of deceptive spirits, are sent by Satan to muddy the waters to make you doubt what's true.

Consistent exposure to lies can damage one's ability to recognize and respond to the truth. Deception is spiritually deadly because, at every point that we believe lies or walk in lies, we cannot accept or believe in the truth, and it is the truth that sets us free, and it is by the truth we are sanctified. When we believe lies, the boundaries designed to keep us on the narrow path are pushed farther away, and then apostasy takes over. Notice how what's false will outweigh what's true in quantity, as 2 Chronicles 18 shows how the 400 outnumbered Micaiah. Mark this down: Error will always outnumber the truth. There will be more who are not legitimately approved than those who are. But we all can place our hope in one thing, which is that truth will always prevail in the end. Time will always be on the side of truth, for Proverbs 12:19 says, "Truthful lips endure forever, but a lying tongue lasts only a moment" (NKJV). A lie has speed, and that's why it's more attractive and believable at any given moment. The truth is not attractive; it's not popular or appealing. It moves slowly, but you will never outrun it. A lie will always be driven by appearances and appeal to emotions because, in reality, it's empty of substance. A lie moves fast to shape its narrative because it's a fabricated one. It tries to get ahead of any truth so that when the truth is finally revealed, it looks weak and defensive.

A false narrative is one in which a complete pattern is perceived, but it is not valid. To remove the context of the story, bits and pieces are deliberately left out. This blurs the message and distorts the truth, yet can result in many buying into a wrong belief. It is a dangerous form of disinformation because the person intentionally leaves out valuable information to mislead others away from drawing an accurate conclusion. Unfortunately, those who live by false narratives are ideal conduits for a lying spirit. They are further made vulnerable due to their lack of true spiritual healing and hidden victim mentality.

The Danger of a Victim Mentality

Spiritual victimization can be traumatic. No true victim should feel the need to trivialize or cover their experience with toxic positivity. However, a victim of a personal or spiritual injury can start to develop a pattern of thinking and responding that's counterproductive and antithetical to the ways of Christ and the healing he offers. If one constantly seeks recognition of one's personal victimhood and ruminates over interpersonal offenses, such rumination can decrease one's motivation for forgiveness and increase the drive to seek revenge. If someone develops a victim mentality which lasts for a prolonged amount of time, they can become so bound by the past that their personal perceptions are the only ones they feel they can trust. In this deceived condition, they place their perception on the same playing field with the Spirit of God and therefore believe how they feel is also how God feels. Their perception becomes their god, which convinces them they are being led by God. Unfortunately, on our Christian journeys, all of us will experience unpleasant things at the hands of Satan, people, and God. From our human standpoint, we will encounter rude, unfair, and unjust things. Because serving him comes with spiritual blows, cuts, bruises, and pain, Christ is our healer. How we process our hurts and respond to Christ's healing determines whether we will be overcomers or victims.

Sadly, many of today's churches have been reduced to acting as philosophical centers specializing in therapeutic methods and New Age healing practices. But the true church is a battleship engaged in a serious battle. It's not an all-expenses-paid cruise ship destined to take us to our desired destination without being disturbed. We cannot serve the Lord faithfully in these Last Days without properly handling insults and injuries. Believers will experience injuries but cannot consistently walk in a victim mentality if the Spirit of God is within them (1 Pet. 2:21–25). We have the same Spirit who raised Christ from the dead in us. We often quote the verse from 1 John 4:4, "Greater is he that is in you, than he who is in the world" (KJV), but do we really believe this? We cannot be victorious and remain perpetual victims.

To reside in a victim mentality is to live below the standards of walking in the Spirit. I once heard a leader say, "The Man who suffered the greatest injustice in history never once spoke of Himself as being a victim. But it's strange to see so many of His followers trumpeting their own victimization as a key ingredient in their identity." Does this sound like many in the church today? A prolonged victim mentality generates deceptive manipulation. This prolonged condition can reveal more about our control issues than the hurt inflicted upon us. In the absence of sanctification and transformation, succumbing to a victim mentality equals calcification. Calcification will eventually cause a spiritual relocation that will move one into spiritual deterioration. Spiritual deterioration will produce bitterness in the heart, which will cause one to constantly look for vindication to cover up hidden vilification.

Satan loves to convince injured believers that they are doing the Lord's work. But God calls people to serve him from a broken place, not from a wounded heart (Isa. 66:2). A victim mentality causes a reversal of the story because it's driven only by personal perspective. It's fault finding that leads to diabolical betrayal. The culprit behind such evil is a lying spirit. It's all about attempting to get you to feel triumphant outside of true healing by causing people to buy into your story and support you by appealing to emotions, hurts, and passions. People who subject themselves to such influence look for Christ to affirm them in the story that they have written or spoken in their displeasure. But Christ is not in the business of endorsing our stories; he is in the heart-transformation business. Unresolved control issues can rewrite a story different from the one God has recorded. With a victim mentality, a person overlooks their own responsibility (where applicable) for healing, while highlighting their misery.

Presumptuous Prophets

It's not just the things they say that don't come to pass or the things they say that do come to pass (Matt. 24:24) that makes a presumptuous prophet dangerous, it is also who they pretend sent them. Jesus said many false prophets would appear and deceive many people. He places this title on those who claim to come in his name but who were never sent. The concept of false prophets was not new. We see them in operation in the Old Testament, and the term has been used to identify those who caused the nation of Israel to fall into apostasy (see 2 Pet. 2:1–2).

Dating back to the days of Moses, false prophets share part of the blame for times of spiritual decline and deception (Jer. 14:11–16). They have been Satan's workers for ages, and Jesus assures us that they will continue to appear until his return. When God's people move backward instead of forward, they have listened to and believed those whom God has not sent. Consider this: God raised the prophet Jeremiah to confront such agents whom God's people embraced (Jer. 28:15–16). God sent him to stop people from developing an ear for deceptive messengers. In essence, when Jeremiah was confronting these fictitious voices, he was up against Satan, who, since ancient Israel, has always used false prophets to move God's people off their intended course. As the saying goes, "Satan has no new games, just different players."

Satan selects men and women with a good presentation, enough truth to be believable, and enough error to be lethal. Perhaps surprisingly, the greatest threat to the church is internal, not external. In Greek, the word for false prophet is *pseudoprophetes*—it describes one who pretends to be sent by God to speak on God's behalf. In Matthew 24, when Christ said that many would come in his name, he was forewarning us of countless individuals pretending to be sent by him. Mark this down: All false prophets desire affirmation, and they are self-appointed, self-driven, and self-aggrandizing. Satan recruits them because they already have a longing for acceptance, popularity, and credibility, which, in many cases, reveals they struggle with rejection issues or hidden jealousy. This desire for affirmation is so deeply rooted in their hearts that it will drive them to practice spiritual plagiarism.

> *All false prophets desire affirmation, and they are self-appointed, self-driven, and self-aggrandizing.*

I heard a pastor describe spiritual plagiarism as the "forgery of the communication and thoughts of another's soul and the characterization of them as one's own in order to boost one's own reputation." New Testament scholar Dr. William Hendriksen once said, "The devil, then, is the very wellspring of lies, the creator of falsehoods… When he lies, he is the original. When he does not lie, he quotes or even plagiarizes; but even then he gives the borrowed words a false setting in order to create an illusion."[1] Yet this dishonest practice does not convict dishonest teachers because it is through this practice that they will wrongly convince others that they are indeed appointed by God. They shamelessly steal messages as if God has spoken to them to "prove" that they are sent by God, which is evidence of the lying spirit working in them. The phenomenon itself is not new, and God has always objected to it. In the book of Jeremiah,

---

[1] William Hendriksen, *New Testament Commentary: Matthew* (Grand Rapids: Baker Book House, 1973).

the Lord said, "I am against these prophets who steal messages from each other and claim they are from me" (Jer. 23:30 NLT).

When the 400 prophets were speaking, it seemed as if God had sent them. Why? Because they were prophesying in his name. God has always taken very seriously how his name is used. While preparing the children of Israel for the Promise Land, he strictly warned them about the danger of taking his name "in vain" (Exod. 20:7). When this phrase is used today, we normally attach it to someone using God's name in a derogatory way. And yes, that usage can be an example of taking God's name in vain, but what God had in mind was the danger of his people attaching his name to things he had never spoken about to validate their personal preferences and ambitions. When people try to speak on God's behalf without heaven's authorization, they become pawns in Satan's hands. They mislead others through demonically inspired or self-invented unscriptural, invalid messages. Whoever is not sent by God cannot accomplish God's will, and neither will he ever come to know it. In Jeremiah 23:21–22, God declared,

> I have not sent these prophets, yet they ran.
> I have not spoken to them, yet they prophesied.
> But if they had stood in My counsel,
> And had caused My people to hear My words,
> Then they would have turned them from
>   their evil way
> And from the evil of their doings. (NKJV)

Not everyone doing a work or service in Christ's name has been validated by the Lord.

There is an order echoed in many scriptures: When God sends you, he will have someone legitimate on earth to acknowledge that you have been sent. This is why, when Nehemiah was accused (Neh. 6:5–9), he was not moved because he had received authorization from the king before starting the project (Neh. 2:2–8). Nehemiah was approved by heaven, so God allowed him to be approved by a legitimate authority on earth. So if people approve of you and they are illegitimate, then that could mean that your work is also illegitimate. See, the Father sent the Son, and the Son has authorization from the Father (John 6:38). Notice, though, that while he was on earth, Jesus' acknowledgment did not just come from himself. God used someone heaven recognized and gave him authority: John the Baptist (John 1:29). We should be concerned and enter serious reevaluation of our position if we find we are connecting ourselves to someone whose work heaven does not even acknowledge.

Acts 16, starting with verse 16, reads,

> Now it happened, as we went to prayer, that a certain slave girl possessed with a spirit of divination met us, who brought her masters much profit by fortune-telling. This girl followed Paul and us, and cried out, saying, "These men are the servants of the Most High God, who proclaim to us the way of salvation." And this she did for many days. (Vv. 16–18 NKJV)

This is Satan's high-level strategic game. Notice that the scripture mentions how much profit she had brought her master from her divination. This implies that she must have been accurate or confirmed many things in people's lives because if she hadn't, she would not be bringing her master much money. Under a demonic spirit, the girl told the people that these men were servants of God. A demon says, "They came to show us how to get saved." The girl, who had never formerly met Paul, was actually saying true things about who he was, whom he was serving, and what his mission entailed.

Usually, we assume that when Satan is opposing a work of God, Satan's counterwork will display some type of hostility or aggression against the servants of God. But Satan has various ways to oppose God's will, and his methods don't all appear evil on the surface. As a church, we need to mature in our understanding of the end times and not be emotionally naïve. Lying spirits that don't appear evil on the surface will distract many from the truth. We have not known or seen the depths of Satan yet. As we get closer to the return of Christ, Satan will meet us in ways we have not previously experienced. Consider Acts 16:

> But Paul, greatly annoyed, turned and said to the spirit, "I command you in the name of Jesus Christ to come out of her." And he came out that very hour. But when her masters saw that their hope of profit was gone, they seized Paul and Silas and dragged them into the marketplace to the authorities. (Vv. 18–19 NKJV)

Why would Paul be "greatly annoyed" if what the girl said was accurate? Paul discerned that her source was not the Holy Spirit. Satan was trying to undermine Paul's work. If Paul didn't deal with the girl, then people would have thought she was believable and that Paul agreed with her source. The girl was practicing spiritual plagiarism. So, when something appears true, we must be careful—it could be stolen. Remember, it's all about the source. Satan will borrow words and place them in a false setting to validate them. This has always been his work.

If we can't discern a true prophet from a false one, then we won't be able to discern what's from God and what's from Satan. Make no mistake: If Satan is bold enough to walk into the garden and deceive, he can walk into your house and mislead. We can't outsmart Satan, who is supernatural. He must be resisted by our submitting to Christ. How could the people know whether Jeremiah or Micaiah was right? Jeremiah prophesied for 23 years, and nothing ever happened in that time. Micaiah's words directly conflicted with the words of the 400. The truth does not always need outside confirmation. Sometimes, time will reveal what is true. But in many cases, when time catches up with what was spoken beforehand, it is too late for a different response. True prophets are authorized to speak on God's behalf because God sent them, and their message will not contradict God's word or nature. In the end, that is its own confirmation.

Chapter 8

The Downfall of Lies

Jehoshaphat's downfall came because he committed himself to Ahab before consulting with God. Even though he made that blind covenant commitment, he later had enough sense not to make another blind leap. He realized that even though God previously granted the rights to Ramoth-Gilead, he still needed to seek the Lord before acting. So, Jehoshaphat put forth the suggestion to Ahab: "But first let's find out what the Lord says" (2 Chron. 18:4). Needless to say, he should have done the same thing before agreeing to join Ahab in the first place.

An important biblical principle is illustrated in Second Chronicles regarding seasons of confusion, seeking answers from God, and spiritual warfare. A principle reflects a truth that forms the basis of something and explains how that thing works or why something typically happens. Principles are not one-off examples; they reflect processes and consequences that happen consistently. So, it's important for us to understand biblical principles. They help us discern right and wrong and influence our thinking to produce right actions. For example, we can learn from what happened to Jehoshaphat when he didn't inquire of God, and we can gain knowledge of how he came to consult 400 false prophets. We can see that if Jehoshaphat had not rejected the 400, Micaiah would not have been consulted.

So, Jehoshaphat's inquiry opened the door for the false prophets to speak, and they were followed by a true prophet of the Lord. Fortunately, Jehoshaphat had enough sense not to function from confirmation bias. Something in him made him ask, "Is there not another?" Sadly, in our post-truth culture, confirmation bias has become the litmus test for how many reach conclusions on whether something is good or evil, true or false. Many seem to follow a thinking pattern like this: "Do I *feel* it's right? Yes, I do. I've researched online, and person X, who has a big following, says it's right. So then, it must be right." We see this in the political world, too. We tend to listen to specific national news channels that support and favor the views we already hold. Our human tendency is to search for information that favors, affirms, and supports rather than rejects or challenges our prejudices. We are prone to interpret evidence in a way that confirms our prior personal beliefs, and we tend to reject or ignore any conflicting facts.

When people are passionate and driven to believe something, they can be persuaded to believe that false things are true, even when evidence is lacking or outright contradictory. Picking only select data that supports our biases is incredibly easy since we live in a digital era with terabytes of facts, studies, analyses, interpretations and opinions that are only keystrokes away. While it's easy to immediately find other people who think like you and agree with you, that does not mean your opinion is correct. Those who live by fallacies often believe they are walking in truth and freedom, while in reality, they are actually prisoners of their own tainted assumptions and cherry-picked support.

On this note, it's helpful to consider the significant differences between the Bereans and Job's friends. One group drew a conclusion based on an unbiased, in-depth investigation into what was being said, and the other drew a conclusion based on presuppositions and external appearances. What were the final outcomes? One was considered more noble-minded than their peers, and the other faced the wrath of God because of their misdiagnosis of what lay before them (see Acts 17:10–15 and Job 42:7). If we can misdiagnose someone's actions, we can also misdiagnose their motives. In 1 Samuel 17:28, we see David's brother misinterpret his motive for coming to the battle. It's interesting that this was the same brother whom Samuel thought was king based on his appearance, but he was not God's choice (1 Sam. 16:6–7). He was angry, perhaps from envy or feeling rejected. So to discover someone's true intentions, one must be willing to do the honest work of an impartial investigation. Reaching a conclusion based on speculation and not investigation is a recipe for a misguided conclusion. Think of the hardened Roman centurion and those with him guarding Jesus after he'd been arrested, presuming Jesus was guilty. However, they change their view when they see the powerful things that happen when Christ dies (Matt. 27:54).

True love takes the time to investigate, while false love only speculates. Most people avoid the hard work of examining a situation exhaustively because doing so might expose their predetermined reasoning; it's easier to defend an erroneous conclusion than to admit you were wrong. We see such behavior in the Pharisees, who were biased in their opinions of Christ. They used propaganda to discourage others from investigating who Christ really was (John 7:45–52). Propaganda is information (often derogatory) used in a biased and misleading manner to promote a particular point of view. It's made up of information or ideas intentionally spread to influence peoples' opinions. Some facts are purposely left out, especially if they contradict or compromise the message being promoted, and only select facts that seem to support it are emphasized.

Propaganda is misleading. In a sense, propaganda is like false prophecy, because false prophecy can bring you to the foot of the cross (make you believe you have the truth) but convince you that you don't really have to get on the cross (in some way, it makes you feel comfortable or validated—like you don't have to make any sacrifice). This is one reason why some dislike the prophetic: it tells us that everything in our lives must display the mark of the cross. Propaganda, unlike true prophecy, advertises and gains followers based on a platform of disinformation. Disinformation controls how you perceive what's being communicated and causes you to misinterpret what you take in. Being misinformed can cause you to believe that something wrong is really right.

> *There is a difference between patriotism and nationalism. Patriotism is care for the country that allows one, without personal biases, to critically diagnose the good and the bad. Nationalism is idolatry that causes elitist, slanted and misleading views of a country.*
>
> *When a culture of people have been shaped to ignore facts, defend blatant lies, jeer at disabilities, and gloat over someone's demise, the destructive sin of nationalism has progressed. This sin is made more egregious when so-called Christians use the name of Christ to promote activities that lead to the instability and fragmentation of a country.*

The dissemination of disinformation is different from and can have more damaging consequences than the dissemination of misinformation. Misinformation can result from accidental untruths, and it's usually easily corrected when one learns the truth. Think of Paul when he was Saul: he was vehemently against Jesus. But as Paul, he is eventually willing to give his life up for Christ. I think 1 Timothy 1:13 says it beautifully: "I was shown mercy because I acted ignorantly in unbelief" (NASB).

Disinformation, however, is created intentionally: it hides its agenda to misrepresent the truth. When those who spread disinformation hear the truth, they reject it and withdraw from those who would question them. In a time when disinformation is increasingly placed before us, we must learn the difference between biblical discernment and suspicion.

What many label *discernment* today really only amounts to feelings and thoughts produced from our own perception, which can eventually lead us to reach the wrong conclusions. Suspicion always begins with the self: it is glorified and gratified by self. Consider when King Saul heard the people praising David. "Saul looked at David with suspicion from that day on" (1 Sam. 18:9 NASB). He was moved to such jealousy that he was willing and determined to kill David. But true discernment begins and ends with God's agenda as the objective standard. In the scheming hands of our adversary, the powerful tools of persuasion and suspicion are not new weapons. They are ancient ones that not only worked in heaven, where he persuaded angels to follow him, but also worked in the Garden of Eden against two individuals who didn't know what sin was. In the Garden of Eden, Satan discovered he could use propaganda to entice us to act against God's will.

While reading our story in 2 Chronicles 18, a thought occurred to me: If Ahab really wanted to know what God was saying, why didn't he initially summon Micaiah with the rest of the 400 prophets (v. 5)? This is what Satan does when he wants to bait you with the absence of the truth first. It's one of his warfare schemes. If Jehoshaphat had initially received the word spoken by the 400, he would not have been aware of Micaiah's existence. His uncertainty with the 400 opened the door for him to hear God's counsel. Ahab concealed Micaiah because he already knew what Micaiah would say, and it wouldn't agree with or be favorable to Ahab (v. 7). Many struggle to discern the voice of God because they have already presupposed what he will say. It's hard to value what God is instructing while also valuing what he hates. Ask Lot's wife (Gen. 19:26). But unless we have already determined not to obey the voice of God, even when it's convicting, his voice is assuring. We can resist lies and avoid downfall if we rest in his assurance.

Chapter 9

Wait on the Lord

It's crucial to learn to wait on the Lord. Learning how to wait is a key to developing spiritual discernment and faith. Discernment and impatience cannot sit at the same table. It takes patience to accurately diagnose spiritual matters, especially those connected to promises. Virtually everything heaven signs off on comes through a waiting period. In essence, waiting is the currency of heaven. As we wait on him, God directs us toward and matures us for the promise (Ps. 27:13–14). You can't separate waiting from faith. Impatient people struggle with this because faith and impatience are incompatible (James 1:1–4). When God develops and matures us through seasons of waiting, even as we earnestly seek his direction, the truth won't necessarily come quickly. Satan knows when we are enduring seasons of confusion or are in the middle of warfare, and he knows that the truth often comes slowly. So if God is developing you through waiting on him and the truth is slow to appear, what might show up first? A lie.

Many confuse time with patience, thinking patience is marked by the duration of time that they have been waiting on God. But no. David said, "I waited patiently for the Lord; he turned to me and heard my cry" (Ps. 40:1 NIV). Faith is the trust and the action of believing while waiting, and patience is what governs your attitude while you're waiting. Faith does not start to grow until you have to wait, and what God permits during the waiting matures you (Ps. 105:16–19). Once you begin to wait, you become stronger and can wait with greater assurance, just as Isaiah wrote, "Those that wait on the Lord shall renew their strength…" (Isa. 40:31 NKJV).

If you are waiting with the type of patience described by David and Isaiah, the more you wait, the stronger you become; but if waiting weakens you, you are not waiting correctly (Josh. 14:7–12). Waiting weeds out superficial people—you have to love God to endure. It tests you to see if you will jump out and believe the lie. It tests your motives to see if you will get angry that others are being rewarded before you. But it's God's way. It's disingenuous to ask God to teach us his ways but get mad when he makes us wait. Our minds will say things that our hearts do not agree with. But in reality, our hearts should be training our thoughts. When you are immature, your mind will influence your heart. Notice when people are carnal and spiritually undeveloped; listen to how they think and talk (Num. 14:1–10). Wrong thinking and destructive speech are magnets for lying spirits. The lie shows up first, so when the truth finally comes, you are left confused. Satan runs with the lie to make you doubt when the truth shows up.

Jehoshaphat is hit with 400 lies first (2 Chron. 18:5). His example reveals that if you can endure lies, you can stand when the truth finally shows up. The truth did not show up until Jehoshaphat was still not sold on the 400th lie. Satan hopes a flood of ungodly counsel will overtake you before God's answer arrives, so beware: you may encounter many erroneous opinions before the truth ever makes its way before you.

You may ask, "If I'm seeking God and God is loving, why would he allow a lie to appear first? Why would he allow me to be perplexed by lies when he knows I desire to wholeheartedly seek and obey him?" Remember: the adversary doesn't want you to know God's will. Such questions are valid, but you can't allow them to convince you that God is being unreasonable, or else you'll leave room for Satan to turn your heart away from trusting God's goodness. God will not permit you to be tempted beyond what you can handle.

There is a difference between what God ordains and what he allows. When God ordains something, it comes directly from his hand. He orchestrates it. But when he allows something, it may come from Satan. God can sign off on whatever Satan comes with because God can use it to develop you. He allowed Satan to touch Job and to sift Peter (Job 1:6–12; Luke 22:31–34). The struggle for us is the question of why would a loving God permit such things? At this point, maturation comes in. You can hinder your maturity by trying to make God like a human. You can't reduce God's love to human love—he is God.

If God's ways are not your delight, the lie from Satan will become your truth. When your heart is pure, Satan will try to distract you with a lie to keep you from holding on until you hear what's true. Satan even tempted Jesus in this way. He said to Jesus, "If you are the Son of God, tell these stones to become bread" (Matt. 4:3 NIV). And how did Jesus respond? He resisted the lies until the truth showed up. And after Satan left him, the angels came and attended him (v. 11). You can't get heaven to show up on your behalf until you first resist what's false. After Jesus passed the test, he went into the city in the power of the Spirit (Luke 4:14). Because he passed this test, he was qualified to function in the Spirit. So, the lie has to come so we may be qualified.

James tells us that if we humble ourselves under the mighty hand of God and resist the devil, he will flee (James 4:7). It doesn't matter how pure your heart is or how much you love God—when you seek him and desire his answers, Satan will get involved. If you don't grasp this concept, you will get angry with God. You'll feel that because your heart is pure, you shouldn't have to endure hardship. Deuteronomy 13:1–3 says,

> If a prophet, or one who foretells by dreams, appears among you and announces to you a sign or wonder, and if the sign or wonder spoken of takes place, and the prophet says, "Let us follow other gods" (gods you have not known) "and let us worship them," you must not listen to the words of that prophet or dreamer. The LORD your God is testing you to find out whether you love him with all your heart and with all your soul. (NIV)

So, God can permit a lie to show up first to test our love for him. Then, to purify his people, God may permit false prophets to function. Therefore, we must be careful before reaching any quick conclusion. Those who are false prophets are eternal enemies of God. When God calls someone a false prophet or teacher, it implies an end result that can't be reversed.

Some people say and teach incorrect things but do so from naïveté or simply out of spiritual ignorance. And through spiritual correction, some might repent and be useable for God's work, like Apollos (Acts 18:24–28). Until there is a confrontation with the truth, it can be challenging to discern spiritual pride from spiritual ignorance—in ourselves as well as in others. We shouldn't expect those confronted with the truth to suddenly, easily change their ways. Think about it: can you name one false prophet who repented in the Bible? There are none. Why? Because false prophets represent God's judgment, they will always have a following among those who don't desire and delight in truth and have abandoned the ways of Christ. God will give people a leader after their own kind. So, he won't get rid of all false prophets. This truth is connected with 2 Timothy 4:3, which says, "For a time is coming when people will no longer listen to sound and wholesome teaching. They will follow their own desires and will look for teachers who will tell them whatever their itching ears want to hear" (NLT).

While the love of God does not prevent the appearance of such false teachers, it does forewarn us about their presence.

Chapter 10

Discerning Dreams and Truth from Lies

THE LYING SPIRIT THAT CAN JUMP INTO THE MOUTH OF A PROPHET is the same lying spirit that can give you a wrong dream. You can desire something so intently that you dream of it. As a pastor, I've heard countless people believe dreams they had were answers to their prayers. However, we have to treat dreams the same way we treat prophecies. They must be tested against God's word and measured by the heart's ambitions (1 Thess. 5:19–21). Jeremiah warned: "Yes, this is what the Lord Almighty, the God of Israel, says: 'Do not let the prophets and diviners among you deceive you. Do not listen to the dreams you encourage them to have. They are prophesying lies to you in my name. I have not sent them,' declares the Lord" (Jer. 29:8–9 NIV). Dreams are prophecies we receive while asleep—and we must discern if they are from God.

If God can communicate the truth to you in a dream, Satan can deliver a lie. Satan's great desire has always been to imitate God's every move and receive worship like God, and his way of attracting worship is through deception. Scholar and author C. S. Lewis said, "There is no neutral ground in the universe. Every square inch, every split second is claimed by God and counter claimed by Satan."[1] Lies show up to influence us to rebel against God. False confirmation and lies cast suspicion on what we once obeyed and surrendered to.

The purpose of the lie is to cauterize one's ability to respond to truth. Every time we believe a lie or walk in a lie, it becomes harder to accept the truth. Lies get you to question and undermine what you once knew was right. So, when you don't know what to do in seasons of confusion, you must be extra vigilant to remain consistent in the truth you already know. Many of us are drowning in confusion because we are looking for something we have not yet heard. Without consistency, you cannot grow in Christ, and your faith cannot fully develop. When Satan becomes more persistent in his pursuit, we must become more persistent and consistent in holding to biblical principles. Keep in mind that if Adam and Eve had remained consistently obedient to the truth God told them, sin could have never entered.

Once you are under the control of a lie, your objective becomes getting others to believe it. Most often, you can receive mercy if you've been deceived. But that mercy becomes limited if you become an author or promoter of deception. This is why the people found more mercy in their deception than the Pharisees did. Paul says,

> I thank Christ Jesus our Lord, who has given me strength, that he considered me trustworthy, appointing me to his service. Even though I was once a blasphemer and a persecutor and a violent man, I was shown mercy because I acted in ignorance and unbelief. The grace of our Lord was poured out on me abundantly, along with the faith and love that are in Christ Jesus. (1 Tim. 1:12–14 NIV)

---

[1] Quoted in *A Mind Awake: An Anthology of C. S. Lewis*, edited by Clyde Kilby (New York: Harvest Books, 2003), 168.

Paul was deceived, and he began to carry out what he had been taught. Yet he still found mercy. So, what's the difference between Paul and the leaders in Matthew 23? For three and a half years, the Pharisees and scribes heard the good news about Christ. As they rejected the truth over a period of time, the mercy available to them became limited. God is just and will not limit mercy if someone has no foundation to understand what is right. For example, Jesus was teaching clearly and candidly among the crowds, but many begin to test his patience through their persistent rejection of his message. Therefore, he adopted a different way of delivering his message through parables (Matt.13:34). Parables concealed the truth from those those who rejected his message and revealed it to those who wanted to hear the truth.

> *Truth erodes where compromise is accepted.*

If God withholds truth because we keep rejecting it, what's left to change us? God showed Ahab mercy time after time; he even gave him the prophet Elijah. But Ahab never turned from his wicked ways; therefore, he became the conduit for the lie.

The lie shows up first because it is designed to get you to rebel against the One who redeemed you and brought you out of bondage. For example, when a person seeks and believes God for a spouse, a counterfeit may show up first. The counterfeit is not necessarily an evil person; they are just not the one. Good things aren't always God things. But what if I take the bait and believe the first person who shows up is the answer to my prayers? How can I disentangle my emotions so I can see that even if someone meets my standards, they still may not be God's will for me? Because Satan's intention is to move us off course, he gets very active when we seek God. It doesn't really matter to him whether we have a sincere desire to do God's will; in fact, if we do, that actually makes him pursue us more. His goal is to make our hearts bitter and cause us to rebel against God's goodness.

Ahab was very clever in not bringing Micaiah forth. He wanted to fulfill his deceptive agenda, and the other 400 prophets would help him achieve it. Ahab needed to deceive others to energize his lie to promote words with no true value. You see, the intent of deception is to exchange something of greater value for something of inferior value. Jehoshaphat had to endure the voices of the majority until the truth showed up. Can we endure Satan's lies until God's truth surfaces? How many confirmations will it take for us to believe? Most people today believe something is true based on one confirmation, but even after hearing 400 confirmations, Jehoshaphat was not sold. He asked for someone else.

Satan has strategic aim, and therefore I must address this biblical truth again: we must be careful before we conclude whether or not something is false or someone is a false prophet or teacher. There is a difference between being misinformed and crossing the line to believing and promoting outright lies. Apollos was misinformed. Aquila and Priscilla pulled Apollos aside to correct him in a way that would give him proper insight (Acts 18:26). But it would be presumptuous to immediately judge someone like Apollos as a false teacher because we shouldn't judge who is illegitimate until after we know whether they have been exposed to the truth. Then we judge by their reaction to it. Are they open to change? Do they change?

Why does Satan specialize in contradicting the truth? To bring confusion. This is why we must understand that when we seek God's will, Satan is going to interfere. Why would he allow clarity and easy, direct access to God? Proverbs 18:17 says, "The first to speak in court sounds right—until the cross-examination begins" (NLT). So the lie (in this case, the 400 prophets) will speak first. Satan hopes the lie convinces you that you don't have to embrace the tiresome process of waiting for God's truth.

This is strategic warfare, and the lie can sound so real. This is not elementary, nor is it something to take lightly. A lie makes itself feel and sound right to convince us that it's really the truth. Why is a lie believable? Because it appeals to the flesh. It confirms and strengthens something in man's fallen nature. It creates a sense of security and confidence. It allows one to live in an illusion to escape the realities of the present. It fortifies one's self-worth and elevates one's sense of importance. But in spite of the self-gratifying promises, at the end of it all, it is a lie. Because a lie's foundation is insecure and based on rhetoric, it never looks to stand alone. To make it seem credible, it recruits others to mindlessly repeat its language.

This is why Ahab was convinced that while one voice would not be enough, surely 400 would work. When a lying spirit is working against you, Satan will use everything at his disposal—he will communicate to you through your thoughts, desires, ungodly counsel, dreams, and coincidences. We see this in the life of Daniel, whose prayer was heard on the first day (Dan. 10:10–15). But then, because there was demonic opposition, it took 21 days for him to receive an answer. Of course, this does not mean everyone will get an answer in exactly 21 days—it can take days, weeks, months, and even years. And after the waiting period, you will realize God was developing you through that time, and you will look back and say, "I see why he didn't answer me at that moment."

It's a spiritual principle that reveals Satan's aversion toward letting us hear truth or receive clarity from God (Acts 13:4–12). And God will measure our love to see if we will endure the lies. Do we love God as much as we tell people we love him?

Many in the church are convinced by popular theological opinions that false prophets are only those who make wrong predictions. But a cessationist who believes the gifts of the Spirit are no longer in operation today can also be a false prophet. How? In the New Testament, a false prophet is equated with a false teacher, so the term applies not only to someone whose predictive gifting lacks accuracy but also to someone who displays a habitual pattern of misusing and misapplying scriptural teachings.

The apostle Peter wrote, "Above all, you must realize that no prophecy in Scripture ever came from the prophet's own understanding, or from human initiative. No, those prophets were moved by the Holy Spirit, and they spoke from God" (2 Pet. 1:20–21 NLT). He was explaining that prophets of old did not conjure up words from the Lord by their own will or reasoning but were inspired and moved by the Holy Spirit. Feelings are not accurate determiners of whether God is speaking. You don't know God by how you feel or what you think—you know him by his word. Peter wrote, "But there were also false prophets in Israel, just as there will be false teachers among you. They will cleverly teach destructive heresies and even deny the Master who bought them. In this way, they will bring sudden destruction on themselves" (2 Pet. 2:1 NKJV).

Peter contrasts those who are true with those who are false, those totally influenced by the Holy Spirit, with those who are moved by fleshly agendas and human imaginations. He also emphasizes the certainty, not probability, of an alarming condition: even as there were holy men of God who spoke as they were moved by the Holy Spirit, there will also be false prophets and false teachers among us today. Notice that God is not going to stop all the false prophets.

Here is the hostility within—*they will be among us*. Satan strategically ensures that these voices do not remain outside the church. The greater danger is always that which is among. Vance Havner once said, "Satan is not fighting churches; he is joining them… Satan does more harm by sowing tares than by pulling up wheat. Satan accomplishes more by imitation than by outright opposition."[2] So Satan says, "I need to imitate to get people to believe in me."

If you want a glimpse into God's heart to see how today's situations will turn out, read about the final years in ancient Judah. The similarities to what is happening in our country today are scary. From political divisiveness to delusion among God's people, there was anarchy in politics and deception all around. We see the same situation in the book of Jeremiah. God's whole point in raising Jeremiah was to turn the people's ears away from that which was false. But Jeremiah struggled with his assignment because whenever one deals with false prophets, one faces the strength of Satan.

We know Nehemiah was doing a work for God because Daniel had already prophesied it (Dan. 9:25). An unseen spirit was using the people Nehemiah lists here: "Sanballat, Tobiah, Geshem the Arab, and the rest of our enemies found out that I had finished rebuilding the wall and that no gaps remained—though we had not yet set up the doors in the gates" (Neh. 6:1 NLT). Nehemiah was not wrestling with flesh and blood; he was contending with people on Satan's payroll. When Nehemiah was getting closer to fulfilling his calling, Satan summoned those listed to keep Nehemiah from completing his task.

> So Sanballat and Geshem sent a message asking me to meet them at one of the villages in the plain of Ono.
>
> But I realized they were plotting to harm me, so I replied by sending this message to them: "I am engaged in a great work, so I can't come. Why should I stop working to come and meet with you?"
>
> Four times they sent the same message, and each time I gave the same reply. The fifth time, Sanballat's

---
[2] Quoted in Dennis J. Hester's *The Vance Havner Quote Book* (Grand Rapids: Baker Publishing Group, 1986).

servant came with an open letter in his hand, and this is what it said:

"There is a rumor among the surrounding nations, and Geshem tells me it is true, that you and the Jews are planning to rebel and that is why you are building the wall. According to his reports, you plan to be their king. He also reports that you have appointed prophets in Jerusalem to proclaim about you, 'Look! There is a king in Judah!' "You can be very sure that this report will get back to the king, so I suggest that you come and talk it over with me."

I replied, "There is no truth in any part of your story. You are making up the whole thing."

They were just trying to intimidate us, imagining that they could discourage us and stop the work. So I continued the work with even greater determination.

Later I went to visit Shemaiah son of Delaiah and grandson of Mehetabel, who was confined to his home. He said, "Let us meet together inside the Temple of God and bolt the doors shut. Your enemies are coming to kill you tonight." (Vv. 2–10 NLT)

Once he realized that Nehemiah would not budge, Satan kept changing his strategy. He eventually went from using outsiders to using someone from within. Shemaiah tried to convince Nehemiah to hide in the Temple of God. But here is the kicker: only priests could go inside the Temple. Not only was Satan looking to move Nehemiah off course, but he also sought to disqualify him. Nehemiah had gone to Shemaiah because he was his friend. But Satan used his friend to try and get him to disobey.

> But I replied, "Should someone in my position run from danger? Should someone in my position enter the Temple to save his life? No, I won't do it!" I realized that God had not spoken to him, but that he had uttered this prophecy against me because Tobiah and Sanballat had hired him. They were hoping to intimidate me and make me sin. Then they would be able to accuse and discredit me. (Vv. 11–13)

How did Nehemiah realize what was happening? Because what Shemaiah was telling him violated the scriptures. Why did Satan fight Nehemiah so hard? Because Jesus can't show up unless the walls are built. Satan was trying to disrupt heaven's rhythm. Notice that Nehemiah used the word *prophecy* (v. 12). In this case, he was referring to the counsel he was receiving. It was not predictive but rather advice on what to do.

We must understand that Satan has goals, desires, and objectives. Satan's desire is to imitate God. Satan's goal has always been to receive worship. And Satan receives worship when God's people are disobedient. Satan offered Jesus great wealth and popularity if he would only bypass God's process. Bypassing God's intended process or course is equivalent to worshiping Satan. I will mention this important truth again: There is a difference between the rewards of Satan and the blessings of God. Satan rewards autonomy, while God only blesses submission.

I find it appalling and alarming that many are preaching and writing books in harmony with Satan's offer to Christ. Offering humankind success and prosperity apart from God's ordained intentions is a scheme devised by the god of this age. If he was bold enough to present a proposal to the King of Glory, how much more would he tempt us? Satan's objective is to take that which is artificial and make it look genuine. This is why deception works: it does not come off as deceptive. We need endurance to wait on the truth because Satan will tell a half-truth to get us to swallow a whole lie. Being patient puts us in a position to recognize the difference, but it requires time and perseverance.

For example, we can't see the difference between the tare and the wheat until harvest time. The two look nearly identical. Consider the parable of the wheat and weeds.

> Here is another story Jesus told: "The Kingdom of Heaven is like a farmer who planted good seed in his field. But that night as the workers slept, his enemy came and planted weeds among the wheat, then slipped away. When the crop began to grow and produce grain, the weeds also grew.
>
> "The farmer's workers went to him and said, 'Sir, the field where you planted that good seed is full of weeds! Where did they come from?'
>
> "'An enemy has done this!' the farmer exclaimed.
>
> "'Should we pull out the weeds?' they asked.
>
> "'No,' he replied, 'you'll uproot the wheat if you do. Let both grow together until the harvest. Then I will tell the harvesters to sort out the weeds, tie them into bundles, and burn them, and to put the wheat in the barn.'" (Matt. 13:24–30 NLT)

This is a powerful parable. Harvest time with God is not always about manifesting a physical blessing. Sometimes harvest is about separating the tare from the wheat. A weed Jesus' listeners would have known was called darnel: it looked exactly like wheat but was poisonous. It would overtake the soil of the wheat and wrap itself around the wheat so tightly as it grew that it was nearly impossible to remove the darnel plant without simultaneously destroying the wheat. So, enduring the frustration, farmers would wait until harvest time because then the distinction between the plants became clear. The darnel stood upright while the mature wheat hung low. Like darnel, Satan does his most severe damage through imitation. An undiscerning eye may not be able to see the difference. It takes God's perspective to separate that which is superficial from that which is authentic.

Satan's lies always promise more freedom than God's will permits. This is why false words seem so believable. Satan works hard to convince us that God's way might not even be true. But if God's way isn't true, Satan wouldn't even try to convince us otherwise.

If Jeremiah was alive today, many would call him a false prophet. People love the Jeremiah who spoke in 29:11 yet discard the Jeremiah who spoke in 29:4. God revealed he was the One who made the people a slave to Babylon; he was behind their captivity. But today, people would say that is not their God speaking. We only want to deal with the God who will give us a future and a hope. The nation at that time was on the verge of collapse. And God desired to reach them because false prophets get active when judgment is underway. Why? Because at the end of the day, Satan wants us to be judged. He wants us removed from God's presence. He doesn't want us to experience what God intends.

The challenge Jeremiah faced is the same challenge prophets face today. How do you teach the concept of surrender to a church culture that feels entitled to freedom? Many misinterpret the voice and will of God due to their idolatry of freedom. This is one reason why questionable prophets will always have the ear of the masses: when liberty and peace are missing in people's lives, and they feel restricted, any words or promises that appear liberating and limitless appeal to their fallen nature (just think about Adam and Eve). But freedom is not a right: it's God-given and God-supervised. It's a gift from God. Freedom without restraints is not liberty. In actuality, it's gross lawlessness. Lamentations

2:14–15 says, "Your prophets have said so many foolish things, false to the core. They did not save you from exile by pointing out your sins. Instead, they painted false pictures, filling you with false hope" (NLT). The prophets prophesied liberty in a place about to experience God's judgment and abandonment. When you set your heart to seek God concerning anything, the false tends to show up first. But if you can endure the lies, the truth will make its way to you. The challenge is to endure without your faith being damaged.

Jehoshaphat ends up incriminating himself because he asks for another prophet with no intention of listening to Micaiah. But God's purpose in allowing Micaiah to speak is for the people. Before Micaiah is taken away, he tells the people to take heed and reveals the counsel of the Lord to them. Why is this important? Due to God's character and nature, he will never leave himself without a witness. No one will stand before his throne and be able to pretend they never knew. Excuses will not tarry in God's presence. He always reveals his will to confront false human reasoning and to give us the way forward.

Chapter 11

Prophecy Provides Heaven's Perspective

Hate will always rest in the bosom of a fool; it should never be found within a believer (Eccles. 7:9). Jesus gave us our marching orders. He warned, "I tell you that anyone who is angry with a brother or sister will be subject to judgment" (Matt. 5:22 NIV), and he directed his disciples to "love your enemies and pray for those who persecute you, that you may be children of your Father in heaven" (vv. 44–45). Being angry with our brothers and sisters—especially when that anger is unjust, when it festers or broods, and when it crosses the border into malice and unbiblical mannerisms—creates more spiritual damage than we can imagine. If we notice hostility growing within us toward others or God, whether from small disagreements or from something that turned to outright anger, we must stop and examine why, for hostility within is evidence something ungodly is at work within us.

In Second Chronicles 18, we see how deeply rooted hostility posits itself against the truth when unjust anger sets hostility in the heart of Ahab. Starting in verse 1, it says,

> Now Jehoshaphat had great riches and honor, and he made a marriage alliance with Ahab. After some years he went down to Ahab in Samaria. And Ahab killed an abundance of sheep and oxen for him and for the people who were with him, and induced him to go up against Ramoth-Gilead. (Vv. 1–2 ESV)

Notice something interesting: from where Jehoshaphat was located geographically, he logically should have gone *up* to visit Ahab, but the text says he went *down*. This detail implies that when one compromises and starts to move outside God's will, one will begin to go down spiritually. Something in Jehoshaphat was changing—he was under the sedation of a seducing (lying) spirit looking to destroy his ending. In order to persuade, this spirit will become increasingly aggressive in its pursuit. A lie does not have substance in and of itself—it's not the truth—so work must be done to convince or influence others that it's right.

We serve a God of instructions. He laid out principles for us to live by in the Bible, and he actively leads us through the Holy Spirit. He has specific plans for us, and when he desires to take us to a certain physical or spiritual location, we must be guided by and abide by his principles. When a principle is rooted and grounded in scripture, it becomes the means by which we should operate and make decisions. This is what makes believers biblical believers. We can't claim to have biblical principles and then have unbiblical practices. If we claim to follow God, biblical principles must govern what we practice and how we live. The will of God and his judgment are always connected to specific locations. The enemy prevents us from going to where God desires us to be; the enemy wants to move us to the place where we will be judged.

If it weren't for Jehoshaphat, we wouldn't see something very significant. Let's examine.

Because he was controlled by a lie, Ahab had no intention of seeking God personally. When you persuade someone to believe a lie, you obstruct their ability to seek God. So when Jehoshaphat said, "I hear you, but let us seek God first," it created a problem for Ahab. Seeking the Lord is a biblical principle. So we should ask ourselves, what does it mean to seek the Lord?

Isaiah tells us to seek the Lord while he may be found (Isa. 55:6). This seeking does not mean praying louder or longer or fasting all day. Rather, the goal is to pray fervently with Christ's agenda governing our focus. Our self-interests should not be at the forefront. Prayer is not only the avenue through which God chooses to reveal his will, it's also the incubator God uses to transform and develop our spiritual growth.

When a lying spirit is present, its objective is to convince you that you have received your answer from God simply because you have heard or seen something that appears to confirm your wishes. Lying spirits use two things in particular to push their purpose: confirmation and the majority's opinion. The appearance of confirmation and the support of majority opinion are persuasive tools, especially under Satan's control. Both play a significant role in today's post-truth culture. This is not anything new: post-truth cultures existed throughout scripture.[1] People have gone along with and supported what agreed with them and their pre-determinations for ages. Jesus' trial sentencing and when the 10 spies' opinions ruled over the two in Kadesh (Num. 13) provide two examples of how listening to the majority can bring undesirable endings.

---

[1] The post-truth movement is actually rooted in the Garden of Eden, where the idea of sin was foreign. The concept of post-truth was crafted by a supernatural being who relied on an exceptionally cunning serpent to carry it out. The Garden was the original dwelling place for the first human pair, Adam and Eve, who were created sinless by God and who dwelled in an environment God called "good." Adam and Eve became the first victims of a post-truth mindset when the Serpent moved them away from a theocentric view of the world to a humanistic one. God, and the authority of his Word, was no longer the centerpiece of their lives; self had become the focus. Self was the new god, and humankind's opinions and feelings had become the new "truth."

As long as something agrees with people's opinion, they will jump on it. And this can lead to spiritual disaster. Second Chronicles 18:6–7 says,

> But Jehoshaphat said, "Is there not here another prophet of the Lord of whom we may inquire?" And the king of Israel said to Jehoshaphat, "There is yet one man by whom we may inquire of the Lord, Micaiah the son of Imlah; but I hate him, for he never prophesies good concerning me, but always evil." (ESV)

This is where blatant hostility enters. Ahab hated Micaiah because he saw him as an opposer. The story continues: "And Jehoshaphat said, 'Let not the king say so.' Then the king of Israel summoned an officer and said, 'Bring quickly Micaiah the son of Imlah'" (vv. 7–8). If Jehoshaphat had not sought God, we would never have come to know Micaiah, nor would we understand Ahab's ability to conceal the truth to get his way.

In German, there is a common phrase: translated into English it says, "Lies have short legs." In other words, they can run fast but not far. Lies eventually collapse because they have no endurance. Usually, a lie will live longer than a liar. But truth endures because truth is who God is. A lie comes to reposition your heart so that when the truth shows up, you won't receive it. This is why some will frame truth-tellers—those who are not in harmony with lies already spoken—as untruthful. They will cause you to start to think that the truth is a lie. But mark this down: God's prophets will never cosign on an untruth.

Evidently, Ahab had past experiences with Micaiah. He already knew Micaiah would not be favorable toward him. Ahab did not believe Micaiah was a false prophet because his words never came to pass: he hated Micaiah because Micaiah's words never confirmed his desires. Micaiah was not shunned because he displayed dishonorable character; he was avoided because he never endorsed carnality. Ahab said, "I hate him." Ahab was a manipulator. By appealing to people's emotions and attempting to block the source of truth, he persuaded others to believe as he did or at least go along with him. But when Jehoshaphat inquired, Ahab knew exactly where to find Micaiah. Though Ahab was controlled by a lie, he knew exactly where to find the truth.

Ahab sent a messenger to summon Micaiah. "And the messenger… said to him, 'Behold, the words of the prophets with one accord are favorable to the king. Let your word be like the word of one of them, and speak favorably'" (v. 12). In other words, the messenger warned, nobody wanted to hear gloom and doom, and Micaiah should not act differently than the other prophets.

> But Micaiah said, "As the LORD lives, what my God says, that I will speak." And when he had come to the king, the king said to him, "Micaiah, shall we go to Ramoth-Gilead to battle, or shall I refrain?" And he answered, "Go up and triumph; they will be given into your hand." (Vv. 13–14)

Notice: a lie will pretend to be submissive to God in public, when in reality, it's already attached to its own agenda. A lie puts on a show to deceive—Ahab knew he had to convince others that he was concerned about God's will, but in his heart, he despised God's way. For someone under the control of a lying spirit, it's all about the show; it's all about appearances. Verses 15–16 say,

> But the king said to him, "How many times shall I make you swear that you speak to me nothing but the truth in the name of the LORD?" And he said, "I saw all Israel scattered on the mountains, as sheep that have no shepherd. And the LORD said, 'These have no master; let each return to his home in peace.'"

Ahab responds in verse 17: "And the king of Israel said to Jehoshaphat, 'Did I not tell you that he would not prophesy good concerning me, but evil?'" Micaiah was not done, though. He continued to prophesy in verses 18–22:

> And Micaiah said, "Therefore hear the word of the LORD: I saw the LORD sitting on his throne, and all the host of heaven standing on his right hand and on his left. And the LORD said, 'Who will entice Ahab the king of Israel, that he may go up and fall at Ramoth-Gilead?' And one said one thing, and another said another. Then a spirit came forward and stood before the LORD, saying, 'I will entice him.' And the LORD said to him, 'By what means?' And he said, 'I will go out, and will be a lying spirit in the mouth of all his prophets.' And he said, 'You are to entice him, and you shall succeed; go out and do so.' Now therefore behold, the LORD has put a lying spirit in the mouth of these your prophets. The LORD has declared disaster concerning you."

This is where the true dynamics are revealed. Without Micaiah, we would not gain a theocentric view of what was really happening. Micaiah reveals what was taking place in the spiritual realm. The people only saw what was happening in the natural. If Micaiah had not spoken, no one would have known the revelation of heaven. We can't know God's perspective from the story until Micaiah shows up. I believe the Lord troubled the spirit in Jehoshaphat, which is why he did not accept what the 400 prophets had spoken. Micaiah's appearance was vital because had he not shown up, the people would have been left with the opinion of the 400. This is why Micaiah says, "If you return in peace, the LORD has not spoken by me. …Hear, all you peoples!" (v. 27).

Keep in mind, Ramoth-Gilead will eventually be the location where God will settle his issue with Ahab. Ahab drags other people along with him. A lie will always try to involve others since it doesn't have enough substance to stand alone.

A lie pulls you close to distort your perspective, but truth from God will cause you to take a step back to gain a godly perspective. If the lie worked on Adam and Eve in the perfect environment of the Garden of Eden, how much more will it work on us currently living in Satan's domain (1 John 5:19)? Human intellect cannot be relied on to properly handle a lie influenced by a supernatural being. If Satan was smart enough to convince a third of angels to abandon heaven, he is powerful enough to persuade fallible humans of just about anything (Rev. 12:4).

God was done offering truth to Ahab, so he summoned someone to bring Ahab to his ultimate end (2 Chron. 18:19). Micaiah appeared in order to leave the people with God's perspective. He brought a theocentric view not to convict Ahab but to offer mercy to the people influenced by Ahab's lie.

> Then Zedekiah the son of Chenaanah came near and struck Micaiah on the cheek and said, "Which way did the Spirit of the LORD go from me to speak to you?" And Micaiah said, "Behold, you shall see on that day when you go into an inner chamber to hide yourself." And the king of Israel said, "Seize Micaiah and take him back to Amon the governor of the city and to Joash the king's son, and say, 'Thus says the king, Put this fellow in prison and feed him with meager rations of bread and water until I return in peace.'" And Micaiah said, "If you return in peace, the Lord has not spoken by me." And he said, "Hear, all you peoples!" (Vv. 23–27 ESV)

A prophetic voice is designed to give a heavenly point of view, and this is what a lie hates. A lie's job is to make people insensitive to otherwise obvious facts, so when the truth comes, they have a hard time believing it. The truth gives you a different perspective because a lie will have you caught up in the now. Truth is driven toward things that are eternal, and therefore long term, while a lie is only concerned with things now. It lives and believes for the moment while the truth builds around those things that are everlasting. God is always concerned about the end (Deut. 8:16). While Jehoshaphat was strengthening the hands of Ahab, someone who did not love God, time was quickly closing in on Ahab and his evil. While God's justice can be slow, it always comes.

> *A lie is concerned with what's now;*
> *Truth is driven by what's eternal.*

Second Chronicles 36:15 says, "And the LORD God of their fathers sent warnings to them by His messengers, rising up early and sending them, because He had compassion on His people and on His dwelling place" (NKJV). Jeremiah 7:13 says, "'And now, because you have done all these works,' says the LORD, 'and I spoke to you, rising up early and speaking, but you did not hear, and I called you, but you did not answer'" (NKJV). In these verses, *rising up early* and speaking emphasizes how the Lord gave his word by the prophets, consistently and with passion. Despite how the people's behavior offended God, he had mercy and sent prophets to warn them, but they still refused him. God speaks over and over because he doesn't want to have to send judgment; he desires to show compassion. What they thought was prophecy not coming to pass was really God showing mercy.

God speaks over and over because once he starts moving, there is no going back (Gen. 7:16). This is a spiritual principle. Second Peter 3:19

explains God's promise is not slack. While people walk according to their lusts, assuming God's promises will never come to fruition, God still shows compassion. Yet we cannot allow time to fool us. We don't want to get to a place where we mock God because he hasn't immediately responded when all the while, he has been granting us time to get right with him.

Deep-seated feelings can indeed be real to you, but that does not mean how you feel reflects absolute truth. If you instinctively believe your feelings are the truth, you shouldn't mind being examined. However, any emphatic conclusion must stand under trial. In fact, you are under another spirit if you think you can freely question or examine God's truth but become outraged when your feelings are questioned.

Just ask Job (38:1–3).

Acts 7:51–52 says,

> You stiff-necked people! Your hearts and ears are still uncircumcised. You are just like your ancestors: You always resist the Holy Spirit! Was there ever a prophet your ancestors did not persecute? They even killed those who predicted the coming of the Righteous One. And now you have betrayed and murdered him—you who have received the law that was given through angels but have not obeyed it. (NIV)

If you keep reading, you'll see that Stephen's life meets an untimely end. Verses 54–60 say:

> When the members of the Sanhedrin heard this, they were furious and gnashed their teeth at him. But Stephen, full of the Holy Spirit, looked up to heaven and saw the glory of God, and Jesus standing at the right hand of God. "Look," he said, "I see heaven

> open and the Son of Man standing at the right hand of God."
>
> At this they covered their ears and, yelling at the top of their voices, they all rushed at him, dragged him out of the city and began to stone him. Meanwhile, the witnesses laid their coats at the feet of a young man named Saul.
>
> While they were stoning him, Stephen prayed, "Lord Jesus, receive my spirit." Then he fell on his knees and cried out, "Lord, do not hold this sin against them." When he had said this, he fell asleep.

Convinced their feelings represented the truth, these leaders vehemently refused to hear anything to the contrary. In doing so, they were opposing the work of the Spirit. How can someone oppose God? One can actively oppose the Holy Spirit through their actions and consistent rejection of the Holy Spirit's works. This is not a moment of temporarily doubting God because of a situation. I am talking about people who intentionally, consistently, and willfully resist and speak evil against God and his works.

When we resist the Holy Spirit, we automatically despise, quench, and grieve him. The Greek word for *resisting* is *antipipto*, which means "to pull against." It means "to oppose by actively rejecting by force." When Luke uses this word in Acts, it's in the present tense, which indicates that the resistance was not short-lived but a habitual practice and lifestyle. It is also in the active voice, which indicates that their resistance was a volitional choice, a choice of free will, that they were not forced to resist. It was not predestined, accidental or by mistake but willful and on purpose.

Quenching the Spirit is as dangerous as resisting God. Paul gives this admonition to the believers in Thessalonica (1 Thess. 5:19). What does it mean to quench the Spirit? It is a metaphor in this text to mean to hinder, repress, stifle, and restrict the Holy Spirit from working and accomplishing his desired task in and throughout an individual's life. As fallible humans, we cannot stop God's will, but we can hinder the Spirit's work in our own hearts and in others. Obstructing the ministry of the Spirit by rejecting and dishonoring the gifts of the Spirit, ignoring his inward promptings, or elevating and substituting our wills above the Spirit's will is, in essence, what quenching the Spirit looks like in operation.

Over the years, there has been an avalanche of misuse of the gifts of the Spirit. And because of unbiblical applications, many have concluded that such workings of the Spirit are no longer needed or valid. Some even go to the extreme of calling modern-day workings of the Spirit "strange fire." Unfortunately, the church has always replaced one error with another error, but just because someone has reframed or abused something doesn't mean God has discarded it. People have abused grace and mercy, but I don't see the church discarding and disregarding their significance.

Inspired by the Holy Spirit, Paul commands us not to despise gifts of the Spirit, such as prophecies, but to test them (1 Thess. 5:20–21). If we are in a place of doubt, before we speak, we should slow down. We should be aware that if we influence others to question God or to doubt that they should hope and believe in him, we can inflict as much harm as those who deliberately misrepresent the Holy Spirit. We shouldn't test the activity or workings of the Spirit based on our subjective experiences, by video clips posted on social media, 30-second sound bites that sound scriptural, or presuppositional teachings from our favorite Bible expositor who makes us feel good about ourselves. If we quench the Holy Spirit, he responds by grieving. When those in Second Chronicles 18 resist and quench the Spirit who speaks through Micaiah, God is grieved—and ultimately, grieving God leads to their demise. So, our goal should be to test things in light of the accuracy of God's word. Without a predetermined stance, we should search the entire context of his word. In that way, we remain open to his perspective and, therefore, truth.

Chapter 12

The Barabbas Age

WHAT WE HAVE WITNESSED DURING THE PANDEMIC—strained relationships, chaos, religious and political fighting—is the result of spiritual forces working behind the scenes. Everything visible and physical around us is preceded by that which is invisible and spiritual. For every action from heaven, there is an opposite reaction from Satan. Once we become biblically oriented, we realize that fixing a natural issue or problem requires first fixing its spiritual cause. Without Micaiah the prophet, we wouldn't have a spiritual or heavenly perspective on the story of Ahab and Jehoshaphat. From this knowledge, we can conclude that we can't fix what's wrong in the fallen, natural world by applying a natural solution. Problems in the natural world that are caused by sin or dark, hidden spiritual influences can only be fully addressed and fixed with a heavenly, spiritual solution. You don't fix the natural by being natural: you fix the natural by being spiritual.

Hostility in a believer's heart becomes a breeding ground for Satan's operation within that believer. The COVID-19 pandemic has revealed hostility deep within the hearts of so-called believers today. If we do not ask God to direct us out of this hostile state, Satan will offer us an enticing but destructive exit ramp. So many of us have experienced disappointment in the wake of the pandemic. We've lost our sense of security. We've suffered death. We've been disillusioned. We've lost trust in politicians, the medical establishment, and churches. We've had disagreements with religious leaders. We've questioned why God didn't do this or that, and these questions tend to breed anger which easily turns to hostility.

> *You don't fix the natural by being natural:*
> *you fix the natural by being spiritual.*

But the issue in the life of believers has never been "*Will* we feel disappointed by God?" We will. We are human, and results don't always go the way we expect, desire, or ask of the Lord. The issue is, "How will we respond when he disappoints us?" If we don't get an outcome we want, will we allow a seed of hostility to take root? Disappointment will either deepen our submission to God or highlight our rebellion. The only person Christ never disappointed or offended was his Father. The longer we walk with the Lord, the more he will disappoint us and offend us. How will we respond?

Christ has caused more offense than any other person who ever lived. Scripture proclaims that he is a sanctuary, stumbling block, and rock of offense (Isa. 8:13–15). If his thoughts and ways are higher than ours, then we can expect to be disappointed at times (Isa. 55:8–9). If the God we serve can never disappoint or discourage us, we are serving a god we fashioned ourselves. He will not always do things we think are acceptable; he will not always show up when we expect him; he will not always stop the things that we believe he should stop, but he will always act based on his goodness. We don't question God's goodness in unexpected gain, but we will question his goodness in unforeseen pain.

The Goodness of God

What is the goodness of God? God's goodness stems from the perfection of his character, which allows him to extend his benevolence toward inferior, created things. His inner excellence amplifies his ability to show mercy, forgive, redeem, and display long suffering. Plenty of verses in the Psalms testify to God not only being good but doing good (Ps. 25:8, 107:1, 119:68). When Moses asked God to show him his glory (his inner attributes), God responded by telling Moses that he would allow his goodness to pass before him (Exod. 33:18–19). Likewise, Paul declares that God's goodness leads men to repentance (Rom. 2:1–4).

When we realize that while we deserve his judgment, he has restrained himself—that should lead us to a changed lifestyle. God's goodness is not always based on positive things happening. Whether we are on a mountaintop or in a dark-valley season of our lives, he is still good. We know we don't deserve his mercy; we don't deserve his grace; we don't deserve his forgiveness; we all deserve his judgment. But he gives mercy, and we therefore know he is good. David sums this up beautifully when he writes, "He does not treat us as our sins deserve or repay us according to our iniquities" (Ps. 103:10 NIV).

When we fail to submit our wills to God's goodness, Satan will offer an exit ramp off the highway of obedience. The offer will be to do what you believe is right and best for yourself in your heart—it's called self-governed living (Matt. 4:1–11). When you enter this place, anyone who opposes what you think is right becomes your enemy. If you see the exit ramp and take it, you may feel relieved and at peace. But that's deception.

***

The story in Second Chronicles 18 shows God about to deal with Ahab once and for all: his mercy has run out. But of course, Ahab has brought other people into the mix, which opens the door for us to meet different characters. Now, we will look at our final two cast members: Zedekiah and God.

The Lie's Spokesperson: Zedekiah

Zedekiah is the leader and spokesperson of the false prophets. (An underlying question we should all ask ourselves is this: Which character have I been like during the pandemic?) Zedekiah was misleading—not only in his view of God but also in his presentation. Zedekiah's name means "God is just," yet he functions and behaves unjustly. So Ahab is under the control of a lie, Jehoshaphat is under the influence of a lie, and Zedekiah is the spokesperson for the lie. Because a lie doesn't have any credibility to stand on its own, it recruits others to do its bidding. Therefore, it needs and seeks out delusional spokespersons. As the spokesperson for the lie, Zedekiah is overdramatic and over-sensational in his presentation and actions. Second Chronicles 18:9–10 says,

> King Ahab of Israel and King Jehoshaphat of Judah, dressed in their royal robes, were sitting on thrones at the threshing floor near the gate of Samaria. All of Ahab's prophets were prophesying there in front of them. One of them, Zedekiah son of Kenaanah, made some iron horns for himself and proclaimed, "This is what the LORD says: With these horns you will gore the Arameans to death!" (NLT)

The spokesperson for a lie will become overly dramatic in their expression to persuade others to believe it. Why? Because a lie's spokesperson will exaggerate points to validate the lie. Lies become believable based on emotion, not truth. You can be passionate about something and still be wrong because passion is not an indicator of truth.

A great illustration of this point happened on January 6, 2021. A mob of over 2,000 protesters stormed the Capitol Building in Washington, DC. They eventually vandalized property and caused bodily injuries and the unfortunate loss of people's lives. The protesters' passion, combined with a lie, caused many to abandon common sense. A number of the protestors have since faced shameful criminal charges. We saw passion under the influence of a lie at the Capitol. Zeal with no real direction from God always breeds disaster.

In Philippians, Paul lists the qualifications that prepared him to be approved by Judaism. They were earmarks that affirmed him and his former ministry. He says:

> If anyone else thinks he may have confidence in the flesh, I more so: circumcised the eighth day, of the stock of Israel, of the tribe of Benjamin, a Hebrew of the Hebrews; concerning the law, a Pharisee; concerning zeal, persecuting the church; concerning the righteousness which is in the law, blameless. (Phil. 3:4–6 NKJV)

Paul said that if anyone should have confidence in their flesh, it should be him. He was a Hebrew of Hebrews, traced back to the lineage of Abraham. In verse 6, "concerning zeal," he persecuted the church. In first-century Judaism, zeal and strong emotions were revered as standards of great character. Having great zeal was the benchmark of someone who possessed the truth, and Paul mentions this insatiable passion in the book of Philippians as well as in Acts 22:3, where he describes himself as "zealous toward God," and in Galatians 1:14, where he says he was "more exceedingly zealous." Having such a background qualified Paul to diagnose his own people in the Book of Romans: "For I bear them witness that they have a zeal for God, but not according to knowledge" (10:2 NKJV).

He knew their condition because he recognized it from his former life. But Paul realized his zeal was wrong. It led him to persecute people and oppose the church that God had ordained. After his conversion, he was willing to die for the same people he had persecuted. Just because you are passionate about something, it doesn't mean you are correct. We can become so passionate that our passion blinds us to truth and influences us to mislead others.

The Barabbas Age

Since the pandemic, unbridled passion over many topics, from masks to medicine to politics to religion, has taken over a large portion of the United States and, sadly, the body of Christ. People have become so opinionated that it often seems rational, reasonable dialog has ceased. We've witnessed the beginning of an age of perverted and inverted zeal: I call it the Barabbas Age. In the story of Barabbas, the people's misguided passion combined with Pilate's desire to be socially accepted worked together to undermine truth for the sake of both parties' emotional affirmation. Persuasion and the desire for social standing work together to undermine biblical standards. Together, they coerce people into feeling like they must make a choice to side with or be against an individual or position. It's an age when prophetic perspectives and eternal principles are suppressed and replaced by misguided and ignorant passions of people so headstrong that it drives them to destructive conclusions. We should be disturbed to recognize what's going on now as we look at biblical parallels. At the crucifixion, the crowd, in passionate vitriol against Christ, chose a known criminal over the Savior (Matt. 27:15–26). Tragically, this was only days after the crowd had cried out, "Hosanna" (Matt. 21:9).

Zeal is fueled by human emotion. Falling prey to error is dangerous because it emboldens the zealous and convinces them they are brave, but that's a result of deception. Think about this: Barabbas' release was the end result of those who believed they were right in that moment. We know Barabbas' name only because of Israel's failed expectations concerning the coming of Christ. They were so focused on a conquering King, that they overlooked the suffering Servant (Isa. 53:1–12). When their expectations for the Messiah weren't met, they became angry, and their anger led to a known and guilty criminal being pardoned. The same was true concerning King Saul. He is mentioned only because Israel no longer wanted God as their king (1 Sam. 8:4–8).

It is sobering to realize some people are in our lives because we struggled to get past failed expectations or didn't want to see things God's way. Allowing raw emotions and misguided feelings that stem from temporary pain and inconvenience to influence permanent decisions is unwise. In essence, the Barabbas Age is a dark period of glorified stupidity. There is nothing more dangerous to God's people than stupidity that is celebrated and admired.

Let me explain what I mean so you can see what's happening in plain view in this country today. History is repeating itself, but are we listening? In the words of George Bernard Shaw referencing Georg Friedrich Hegel, "We learn from history that men never learn anything from history."[1] It is a privilege to be a citizen of this country, but I tremble at the acceleration with which the nation is abandoning God. George Mason, the father of the Bill of Rights, once said, "A nation can not be rewarded or punished in the next world. So, they must be in this world. By a lot of change of events and cause and effects, God

---

[1] From Bernard Shaw's *Heartbreak House* (Edinburgh: R. and R. Clark, Ltd., 1949), 37.

punishes national sins by national calamities."[2] Studying how God dealt with nations in the past has led me to conclude his hand now judges this nation.

The Dangers of Spiritual Stupor

A common denominator that previous empires experienced during the ends of their reigns is one we now see in the United States: a stupor permeates its citizens. What is *stupor*? The meaning is both natural and spiritual. The expression is used in the Old and New Testaments (Isa. 29:9–12; Rom. 11:8). Both accounts show that God was the author of the judgment, which was in response to the peoples' habitual, rebellious acts. The spirit of stupor marked God's judgment against peoples' ongoing sin.

From a natural point of view, *stupor* is the suspension of the ability to be sensible. It is the suppression of sense and feeling due to a lack of attention to one's best interests. From a natural perspective, it's when plain common sense and facts take a backseat to political persuasion, personal interests, propaganda, and posturing. King Solomon, under the inspiration of the Holy Spirit, wrote, "History merely repeats itself. It has all been done before. Nothing under the sun is truly new. Sometimes people say, 'Here is something new!' But actually it is old; nothing is ever truly new" (Eccles. 1:9–10 NLT). Do we really believe this? Some may argue that modern advances in technology and medicine prove the statement false, but that's not the biblical meaning of the expression, "there is nothing new under the sun." The expression reflects how the cycle of human life on earth repeats itself. Regardless of new inventions, a new calendar year, and human actions, responses to and consequences of actions have been and will remain consistent. The technological advancement of a culture will never suppress or hide the pattern of

---

[2] Quoted in James Madison's *Debates in the Federal Convention of 1787* (Ohio UP, 1987).

humankind's depraved inclinations. In actuality, the rise of technology has magnified humankind's sin.

> *While many are focused on the impact climate change could have on the world, many are overlooking a more perilous version of change. Social climate change creates a hostility within, the path of which is hard to redirect. Every great kingdom has become vulnerable to external calamities when its people, structure, and values started to deteriorate from within. Nations cannot be judged in the afterlife; they are judged in real time.*
>
> *Consider the prophetic words of Abraham Lincoln in his 1838 Springfield, Illinois speech: "At what point then is the approach of danger to be expected? I answer, if it ever reach us, it must spring up amongst us. It cannot come from abroad. If destruction be our lot, we must ourselves be its author and finisher. As a nation of freemen, we must live through all time, or die by suicide." Lincoln stated that if we as a country (the US) would ever be destroyed, destruction would come from within. It's happening before our eyes. We are so driven by the present we don't see that history is coming to pass.*

What we see today is nothing new; this has happened before. Things seem new to us when we have never personally experienced them, but understanding history can keep us from being blind and misled in the present. We have a historical example in Germany during World War II. While awaiting execution in a prison cell, the late Dietrich Bonhoeffer recorded his thoughts. His notes were collected in a work we now know as *Letters and Papers from Prison*. In one of those papers, he wrote about what he believed gave rise to the acceptance and adulation of Hitler. In a subsection entitled "On Stupidity," Bonhoeffer argues that stupidity is a more dangerous enemy of the good than malice. He explains: "One may protest against evil; it can be exposed and, if need be, prevented by use of force . . . against stupidity we are defenseless. Neither protests nor the use of force accomplish anything here; reasons fall on deaf ears." He continues,

> Facts that contradict one's prejudgment simply need not be believed – in such moments the stupid person even becomes critical – and when facts are irrefutable they are just pushed aside as inconsequential, as incidental. In all this the stupid person, in contrast to the malicious one, is utterly self-satisfied and, being easily irritated, becomes dangerous by going on the attack. For that reason, greater caution is called for when dealing with a stupid person than with a malicious one. Never again will we try to persuade the stupid person with reasons, for it is senseless and dangerous.[3]

Bonhoeffer then sums up his analysis of how the adoration of Hitler depended upon the stupidity of the people. He concludes,

> The fact that the stupid person is often stubborn must not blind us to the fact that he is not independent. In conversation with him, one virtually feels that one is dealing not at all with him as a person, but with slogans, catchwords, and the like that have taken possession of him. He is under a spell, blinded,

---
[3] From "An Account at the Turn of the Year 1942–1943: After Ten Years," in *Letters and Papers from Prison*, translated by Barbara and Martin Rumscheidt. *Dietrich Bonhoeffer Works*, Vol. 8 (Minneapolis, MN: Fortress Press, 2010), 43.

misused, and abused in his very being. Having thus become a mindless tool, the stupid person will also be capable of any evil and at the same time incapable of seeing that it is evil. This is where the danger of diabolical misuse lurks, for it is this that can once and for all destroy human beings.[4]

Does Bonhoeffer's description sound familiar? It describes precisely what we are seeing take place in the US now. We are no longer dealing with common sense and sensible reasoning; we are battling political partisanship, slogans, and trending catchphrases. Bonhoeffer's prophetic words are as valid today as they were when he wrote them over 75 years ago.

From a spiritual viewpoint, stupor can be a byproduct of what I call "providential hardening" by God. Providential hardening happens when an individual or nation persistently rejects the conviction and warnings of the Spirit. In return, God allows a spiritual hardening that causes apathy toward, disconnection from, and disillusionment concerning the things of God. Think of Pharaoh: contrary to popular teachings that misuse Romans 9 to teach that God arbitrarily hardened Pharaoh's heart, the truth is God hardened his heart only after he refused to respond to God's voice through Moses (Exod. 8:15,19,32). Therefore, the thought that Pharaoh could not respond is untrue, and it creates an unbiblical view concerning God's character. The Bible clearly states in numerous verses that Pharaoh's hard heart was a result of his own rebellion (Exod. 7:13,22), and not because God was the *cause* or the *author* of it. His repetitive rejection of God's instructions led to a "providential hardening." In this condition, a person or a nation appears to be in a spiritual coma-like state due to their lack of ability to respond to or comprehend God's commands. As a result, an appetite for righteousness is replaced by an uncontrollable desire for sensual pleasures.

---

[4] Ibid., 44.

Vivid pictures of such stupor are found in Noah's and Lot's days. Christ warns us that these cultures, which in scripture are considered to have been part of the two worst periods in humanity's existence, will be combined into one right before his return (Luke 17:26–30). The people in those two cultures were numb, blind, spiritually desensitized, and insensitive to the word of God. The Lord tells us, "It will be just like this on the day the Son of Man is revealed" (Luke 17:30). In the pursuit of happiness, right before the Lord's return, people will love who they are and live their "best lives." It is very alarming that these moments determine humankind's eternal existence, and when they burst upon the scene, they will be anything but business as usual.

Being callous and dull-hearted concerning the things of God turns one into being what the Old Testament calls *foolish* or *stupid*. The two words are used interchangeably throughout the book of Jeremiah (4:22; 5:4,21; 10:12,21). In Hebrew, the word for stupid or foolish is *e-veel*. It doesn't describe low intelligence. Instead, it means one who is stupid by choice. It reflects the state of mind of people who pervert their logic to justify what they know is false. If one is *e-veel*, they have chosen to believe things that contradict common sense.

Under this delusion, people justify what common sense tells them is wrong through distorted logic. We see the concept in the New Testament when Paul confronts believers in the region of Galatia. Paul uses the Greek term *anoetos,* or foolish, to address believers who were being persuaded to believe another gospel that introduced a different Jesus (Gal. 3:1–3). The term refers to those unwilling to use their mental faculties to understand what they know to be right or correct. It's not applied to people who cannot understand but to those who think carelessly due to external influences. It implies they have refused to slow down and think things through. Instead, they have allowed flattery and emotion to override what they clearly once knew was true. By their own free choice, the Galatians were walking in stupidity.

The fallout of the post-pandemic era has seen a shift in the hearts of many who proclaim that Jesus is Lord. It seems as if scales have developed over people's eyes such that reasoning from the scriptures has been supplanted by philosophical rationalizations that have nothing to do with Christ or his purpose for his church. I find that when I remind many of their former confessions and their commitment to live according to the standards of the Bible, I am met with irrational rhetoric and vehement displeasure.

Three questions Paul proposed to believers in Galatia are still valid today:

- "Who has bewitched you?"
- "Have I now become your enemy by telling you the truth?"
- "You were running a good race. Who cut in on you to keep you from obeying the truth?"

We need to be challenged in this hour despite the vitriol that comes with being under a spiritual stupor. A profound verse highlights the urgency of the time when Samuel was called, and I believe it applies to us now: "The lamp of God had not yet gone out…" (1 Sam. 1:3). In the midst of a culture marked by spiritual backsliding and apathy, God spoke to Samuel before the light was extinguished. I pray that we, like Samuel, may awaken to the voice of God while there is still time. Let us never forget that Satan vehemently promotes lies, and passion is only good under the influence of God and his truth (John 2:17).

Chapter 13

The Countdown to Finality

Zedekiah is deceptive, disrespectful, and delusive. His name means "God is righteous or just," but he treats God's prophet with injustice and God's truth as if it were a lie. The nature of his character is apparent: "Zedekiah son of Kenaanah walked up to Micaiah and slapped him across the face. 'Since when did the Spirit of the Lord leave me to speak to you?' he demanded" (2 Chron. 18:23 NLT). The character of the spokesperson for the lie is clear. Slapping someone on the cheek insults and shames that person. An advocate for a lie displays mannerisms that reveal a lack of fear of the Lord. How is that? Because the opposite of the fear of God is scorn.

To *scorn* is to belittle the authority or the character of someone. It is to disregard God's ruling authority and the earthly authority he establishes. It means showing extreme contempt and disdain. That attitude springs from a person's opinion of an object. Someone who is scornful seeks to undermine true wisdom by expressing an opinionated and suspicion-arousing view of things to convince others to follow his or her derision.

Of course, we all have opinions, but having opinions is different from acting in an opinionated manner. The scornful are so driven by their opinionated self-righteousness that when others do not believe them, their speech and actions become destructive.

Psalm 1:1 warns of the danger of sitting in the seat of scornful people: we can be assured that if we don't, we will be blessed. The day will surely come when God will deal harshly with the scornful (Prov. 3:34). When Zedekiah's view is contradicted by truth, he responds in his flesh and targets Micaiah, looking to embarrass him. A spokesperson for a lie will lash out at others.

What is in people that finds harmony with Satan that he picks them? Often, spokespersons have a history of anger, rejection, and belittling others, and their hearts seek vengeance and validation. Moments of desperation, chaos, and confusion create a market for those seeking to be validated. But watch Micaiah's reply: "You will find out soon enough when you are trying to hide in some secret room" (2 Chron. 18:24).

The story is interesting here because we don't know what Micaiah is referring to, but we know he is in a foretelling mode, speaking of what is coming. Consider that Ahab, the person under the control of the lie, will meet his death at Ramoth-Gilead. And Jehoshaphat, as the person under the influence of the lie, will meet God's mercy. So, a day of judgment is coming for the lie's spokesperson. While Zedekiah does not die at Ramoth-Gilead, a day is coming when he won't escape. So, the spokesperson can look like he or she is thriving, prosperous, and living a life of fulfillment, but in reality, their day is coming. It has been determined by God and can't be altered. We don't know exactly how the story ends for Zedekiah, but we can assume that Micaiah's prophecy didn't fall to the ground. Zedekiah paid to be a spokesperson for the lie.

Responses to Discouragement and Disappointment

Before we consider the character of God, we need to think about something. If we are unwilling to surrender to God when our hearts are bitter, hurt, and offended, we can fall into destructive ways of thinking and practices. Plenty of messages have been given about the children of Israel building the golden calf, but not many about what led them to do it. In a season of failed expectations, the children of Israel became agitated and discouraged. In that context, they built the golden calf (Exod. 32:1–35).

Seasons of confusion can produce discouragement that, unchecked, will lead to doubt in God's care and sovereignty. But we must understand that God will allow us to experience great disappointment and discouragement to test and measure our submission. He uses disappointments to redirect our misguided expectations and desires. He uses rejection to direct and redirect us, while Satan uses it to damage us. We must be aware: if we think we serve a God who never disagrees with us or disappoints us, then the god we serve is ourselves.

In seasons of spiritual disappointment, we should ask ourselves several questions.

- How do I respond when my hope is shattered?
- How do I respond when I disagree with God?
- How do I function when God has discouraged me?
- How do I feel when God tells me *no*?
- Do I desire comfort or clarity?
- Am I focused on speed or direction?
- Who am I doing this for?
- What am I living for?
- Am I focused on my happiness or the glory of God?
- Who is the author of my story?

- Am I driven by results or what's next to my name in God's book?

Sometimes, God will tell us no and not explain why. This is a hard pill to swallow. We want an explanation. We want to know why and feel like we can't move forward unless we understand the reasons. Not submitting our hearts to God during these challenging moments draws the attention of Satan, who loves to fish in the hearts and thoughts of those who are distracted and disturbed.

A mind that doesn't view life through the lens of the scriptures becomes a breeding ground for deception. Satan will use our thoughts and misperceptions as an incubator for wrong decisions. A dishonorable thought life will cause one to neglect God's known will, despise his revealed will, and pursue one's own will. Eventually, the mind in this state becomes suitable and attractive for the works of demons. If we see our personal desires as a priority and God's will as optional, it's a good indicator our minds have come under demonic assault. Refusal to surrender an expectation elevated above God's intention is the beginning of a slippery slope. An unwillingness to surrender and submit our misdiagnosed expectations leads to hearts being unresponsive to the Spirit of God's command.

Judas' heart was like this: because his expectation was greater than his willingness to concede, he betrayed Christ. Perhaps the most vivid example of a tragic misinterpretation of prophecy occurred in the life of Judas Iscariot. His misconceptions about the coming of the Messiah resulted in the betrayal and death of Jesus and his own death by suicide (Matt. 27:5; Acts 1:18). If Judas had not misinterpreted prophecy, he probably would not have done what he did.

In reference to Judas belonging to a radical sect, Richard T. Ritenbaugh explains:

> Though motivated primarily by socio-economic and political factors, the Zealots also had prophetic ideas driving them. They believed that if they turned Israel back to God and incited war against the Romans, the Messiah would arise to lead them and establish his Kingdom. This "understanding" resulted from misinterpreting many prophecies concerning Christ's comings. In short, the Zealots ignored many of the prophecies regarding His first coming and completely mis-timed those about the second.[1]

There are essentially two choices to make when we disagree with God: we can enter into deeper submission to him, or we can choose a life of open rebellion. Disagreement can lead us to a deeper appreciation of his sovereignty or cause us to despise his wisdom and goodness. Despising God's wisdom leads to a heart that is constantly hostile to God's ways and plans. To persevere in a way that will please God, we must submit three things to the Holy Spirit's influence: our mentality, emotions, and responses. Failure to surrender these will cause us to pursue idols who will function as our "new" god because we were discouraged by the "old" God.

Satan will always provide a substitute when we are discouraged and irritated with God. For example, when the Israelites felt discouraged by God, they turned their discouragement, criticism, and resentment toward Moses (Num. 14:1–4). This pattern is repeated throughout the scriptures: when people are angry at God, they carry out their frustration toward the person God is using or the person who has received authority from God. To convince others that a message is illegitimate, all an angry person has to do is shame and find fault with the messenger. Fault-finding and blame are ancient strategies of Satan.

---

[1] "No Private Interpretation," *Forerunner: Preparing Christians for the Kingdom of God*, May 1997. https://www.cgg.org/index.cfm/library/article/id/354/no-private-interpretation.html.

It's hard to attack a biblically supported message, so to discredit the message, one must create doubt concerning the messenger. While God was revealing his instructions to Moses to help direct the people, they became disinterested and despondent (Exod. 32:1). In response to the divine delay, they showed displeasure with Moses. So, they made a god to take them where they wanted to go. It's interesting how idolatry works. It's the same pattern Satan used in heaven. Because he was not a creator, he could not be independent. So, he took the angels God created to support his insubordination. His tail drew a third of what God had created to support his planned coup.

Satan will always look to take what God has done, given, and who God has rescued and use it or them to underpin his agenda and goal. Satan persuades those he did not create to underwrite his rebellion. So, too, did the children of Israel: they took their plunder of Egyptian riches to fund their own rebellion. God allowed the Jews enough wealth to replenish them after 400 years of slavery and build his tabernacle in the wilderness (Gen. 15:13–14, Exod. 35:4–29). As they became discouraged, however, they took the gold God had given them to finance idolatry. People in idolatry will take what does not belong to them to finance Satan's agenda. But when people associate themselves with a lie, they have a lot to lose. A lie never has lasting substance.

Captive to Satan's Will

The first time a concept is mentioned in scripture is important. Many call it the law of first mention. It implies that to fully understand a word or belief, we must go to the place in the scriptures where it's mentioned first. So, it's not a coincidence that we have the story of Cain and Abel. Because they are the first two naturally born individuals, through them, we gain an understanding of what obedience, righteousness, murder, blood, and anger really entail. We must understand Cain because the characteristics shown through him will be present in the church in the Last Days.

Cain murdered his brother because he could not handle being disappointed by God (Gen. 4:6–8). Cain's hostility ran so deep that he could not hear God's desire for mercy; instead, he only heard rejection. First John 3:4–9 says,

> Whoever commits sin also commits lawlessness, and sin is lawlessness. And you know that He was manifested to take away our sins, and in Him there is no sin. Whoever abides in Him does not sin. Whoever sins has neither seen Him nor known Him. Little children, let no one deceive you. He who practices righteousness is righteous, just as He is righteous. He who sins is of the devil, for the devil has sinned from the beginning. For this purpose the Son of God was manifested, that He might destroy the works of the devil. Whoever has been born of God does not sin, for His seed remains in him; and he cannot sin, because he has been born of God. (NKJV)

Notice that 1 John 3 is layered with present-tense actions. So, whoever abides in him does not make a practice out of sin. The verses continue,

> In this the children of God and the children of the devil are manifest: Whoever does not practice righteousness is not of God, nor is he who does not love his brother. For this is the message that you heard from the beginning, that we should love one another, not as Cain who was of the wicked one and murdered his brother. And why did he murder him? Because his works were evil and his brother's righteous. Do not

> marvel, my brethren, if the world hates you. We know that we have passed from death to life, because we love the brethren. He who does not love his brother abides in death. Whoever hates his brother is a murderer, and you know that no murderer has eternal life abiding in him. (Vv. 10–15 NKJV)

Cain essentially became a prisoner of hate, and because of this, he carried out what the evil one desired, which was murder. Over time, Cain's perceived rejection by God led to Satan being able to work on Cain's mind, which led him to harm his brother. So, when God speaks to Cain, Cain retorts, "Am I my brother's keeper?" (Gen. 4:9). The same attitude will be among those in the last-day church. Rejection can cause people to become so unified with an unhealthy temper that God's counsel cannot recalibrate their emotions.

Jude 3 says, "Beloved, while I was very diligent to write to you concerning our common salvation, I found it necessary to write to you exhorting you to contend earnestly for the faith which was once for all delivered to the saints" (NKJV). Jude was not writing to unbelievers; he was writing to believers. "The faith" refers to a body of doctrine given by the Holy Spirit. We have to jump into the battle and contend with a hostile enemy. We can't continuously sit on the sidelines and allow a spokesperson to spew lies while we do nothing. Granted, there are times to speak and times the Spirit instructs us to be quiet (Eccles. 3:7). Learning to be led by the Spirit is paramount in knowing when God approves you to speak. God will put us in situations where the truth we know goes against what a person speaking for a lie is saying. A lie will always want to take the floor because it doesn't have its own substance.

When a believer is not contending for the faith and remains silent, the lie will take the microphone. Jude 4 says,

> For certain men have crept in unnoticed, who long ago were marked out for this condemnation, ungodly men, who turn the grace of our God into lewdness and deny the only Lord God and our Lord Jesus Christ. (NKJV)

These men are spiritual terrorists who blend in until it's time for them to carry out their plan. They will not make a scene before their time; they will first appear as "law-abiding citizens." But then, once their plan is carried out, the innocent are stunned because they never thought the people were terrorists to begin with.

The Greek word for "crept in" is *pareisduno*. It means settling down alongside those already there—in other words, joining something under false pretenses. This type of deception is solely an inside job. They creep in because a door has been left open. But there is also a secondary meaning: they "creep in unaware" because they are seductive and believable due to the cleverness of their speech, and their non-threatening appearance. Because they are so clever, they have a way of twisting scriptures to cajole you to abandon a viewpoint you knew was correct and convincing you to agree with them and join their views. Who are these individuals? God already knows what their charges will be at the seat of judgment. But what causes them to be condemned by God?

First, they are ungodly. There is a difference between the righteous, the ungodly, and the sinner (1 Pet. 4:18). The ungodly lack interest in the ways and word of God. And because of this, their attitude shows a lack of reverence. These are the same people Asaph struggled with in Psalm 73. Righteous people jump into the word of God, and their delight is in the law of the Lord. Asaph struggled with people who did not delight in God's ways, yet their lives were prosperous. The ungodly use God's grace as a license to pursue their desires and serve their fleshly appetites.

They disregard and refuse to acknowledge the only Lord God and his rule over them.

Jude 11 says, "Woe to them! For they have gone in the way of Cain, have run greedily in the error of Balaam for profit, and perished in the rebellion of Korah" (NKJV). *Woe* is a denouncement on those who once had privileges and abused them. So why does God use Cain's name in the book of Jude thousands of years after Cain's death? Remember that most of the disciples were dead by the time Jude was written; therefore, the leadership of the church was changing hands. When a new generation assumes leadership, the community is vulnerable as change creates opportunities for Satan's schemes. The Holy Spirit is reminding us that as we get closer to the return of Christ, we will see Cain's character in the lives of many. We will find his character not only in the church but also the personalities of Balaam and Korah.

Jude did not explain who these people were. Neither did Jesus, who said, "Remember Lot's wife" (Luke 17:32). Why? Because their audiences knew the individuals mentioned. What's interesting about the characters listed in Jude is that they all rebelled against God after a particular truth had been revealed. Rebellion, the willful rejection of God's known will, is the most regrettable charge that can be laid upon a believer. It's an intentional abandonment of what God has said to pursue what one desires. We begin to rebel when we allow our will to become dominant over God's commands (1 Sam. 15:22–26). A person who refuses to be subject to God's given order becomes unruly and disorderly. Their attitude indicates unresponsiveness to God and an inability to receive anything that doesn't correspond with their personal intentions. That person has become spiritually unconscious or dead. Instead of being connected to God, a rebellious person's spiritual senses are essentially in airplane mode—warnings and instructions are going out, but nothing is coming through. When God sees rebellion, he sees

Satan. The last thing any believer would want is to be associated with character traits similar to Satan's.

How do we know these people are going to be in the church? Jude verse 12 says, "These are spots in your love feasts, while they feast with you without fear, serving only themselves. They are clouds without water, carried about by the winds; late autumn trees without fruit, twice dead, pulled up by the roots" (NKJV). This verse mentions "love feasts," which took place among believers. There are those who will feast with you yet have no fear of God; they only desire to serve themselves. Verse 19 says, "These are sensual persons, who cause divisions, not having the Spirit." There is a truth here that's important to mention. He calls these individuals sensual and void of the Spirit. What does this mean? The Greek for *sensual* is *psychikos*. It indicates one who lives according to their physical senses and develops an affinity and a desire to live a life governed by soulish affections. James 3 warns us of sensual individuals who pretend to have wisdom and give counsel, but their advice is not from God. It's demonic and of this world (v. 15). Such individuals do not live or walk by the Spirit of God. They live like animals; they are only subject to their own appetites and passions; they are instinctive, divisive, delusional, and dangerous.

As Satan gains entry into a person's mind, he will take the person captive to do his will. We would do well to consider 2 Timothy 2:24–26 for Paul's advice on avoiding and escaping the devil's snare:

> And a servant of the Lord must not quarrel but be gentle to all, able to teach, patient, in humility correcting those who are in opposition, if God perhaps will grant them repentance, so that they may know the truth, and that they may come to their senses and escape the snare of the devil, having been taken captive by him to do his will. (NKJV)

The Character of God

Back in Second Chronicles 18, we get to the most important person in the story—God. Without his perspective, all is meaningless. God cannot be just unless his way is revealed. I believe that Micaiah's appearance has more to do with God's justice than it has to do with Jehoshaphat's initial rejection of Ahab's prophets. By revealing his intentions through Micaiah, God makes his standard known. He is always merciful enough to reveal his way. How we respond to his mercy determines the consequences. Verses 18–22 say,

> Then Micaiah said, "Therefore hear the word of the LORD: I saw the LORD sitting on His throne, and all the host of heaven standing on His right hand and His left. And the LORD said, 'Who will persuade Ahab king of Israel to go up, that he may fall at Ramoth-Gilead?' So one spoke in this manner, and another spoke in that manner. Then a spirit came forward and stood before the LORD, and said, 'I will persuade him.' The LORD said to him, 'In what way?' So he said, 'I will go out and be a lying spirit in the mouth of all his prophets.' And the LORD said, 'You shall persuade him and also prevail; go out and do so.' Therefore look! The LORD has put a lying spirit in the mouth of these prophets of yours, and the Lord has declared disaster against you." (NKJV)

Micaiah has two prophetic visions, and both reveal the coming judgment to Ahab. They are similar to the visions in the books of Job, Zechariah, Daniel, Isaiah, and Revelation. Only in these books and Micaiah's visions do we see the throne of God. These are the only moments that God parts the curtain and allows us to see what's normally hidden.

In the first vision, Micaiah sees Israel wandering like sheep without a shepherd (v.16), which describes a nation without a leader. Jesus uses the same terminology when he sees people walking hopelessly and aimlessly in his day (Matt. 9:36). If Micaiah's first vision is like the appetizer, the second vision is the entrée.

The second vision explains how the first vision will happen. The vision reveals the power of God, surrounded by the hosts of heaven. It reveals that not only good angels are in God's presence, but also the fallen. The spirit mentioned in the verses reveals a specific spirit, not just any spirit.

People tend to get confused when God tells the lying spirit to go and that he will succeed (v. 21). But this happens for a reason. God permits the lying spirit to prevail because Ahab is determined to do evil. God has an issue with Ahab, and in return, Ahab has an issue with the truth.

There is a difference between what God approves and what he condones. He ordains the things that come directly from him to perfect our character and mature our faith. But there are things God will permit that are against his character. However, he uses them to push his agenda forward. Think of it this way: God will never associate himself with murder. Still, to fulfill the penalty of sin, God allowed a murder to accomplish his will when he allowed Jesus to die on the cross for the sins of humankind (Acts 2:22–24).

What we see happening now in the wake of the pandemic has been in the works for years. This is not a one-time situation where God is fed up because of one thing. God wasn't fed up because Ahab did one thing wrong. No, God had reached a place of no return in reference to how he would deal with Ahab. Ahab's sins had reached a place of finality with God.

But here is the million-dollar question: Why would a loving God, full of compassion, allow or permit a demon (a lying spirit) to succeed? A biblical principle provides an explanation. When an individual has reached a point of no return, God will allow the effects of what sin has caused to take place. He will permit the people's or nation's choices to be the instrument of their own judgment.

For example, in 1 Samuel 8, God allowed Saul to be king even though Saul wasn't God's preferred choice. Despite the prophet Samuel's efforts to convince the people to hear things from God's perspective, his voice was dismissed and rejected. When people want what they want, it doesn't matter how you try to reason with them—all they want to hear are words that affirm and confirm their own wishes. It is hard to value and obey what God instructs while valuing the things you prefer—think of Lot's wife, who could not respond to mercy because she valued what God had rejected (Gen. 19:13–26). She devalued divine counsel and held her own choice in esteem. Therefore, while she was allowed to escape Sodom, her final ending was the same as those who perished in Sodom.

Until your heart becomes driven by that which is eternal, everything in this world will become your treasure (Matt. 6:19–21). Saul was what the people desired, and God didn't oppose it. Instead, he allowed them to have a king from the tribe of Benjamin even though a king was supposed to come from the tribe of Judah (Gen. 49:10). God gave them an illegitimate king because their hearts no longer desired the true King.

Degrees of Deception and God's Wrath

There are five consecutive levels or degrees of deception.

- First, when Satan himself deceives you;
- Second, when you are deceived by others;

- Third, when you are deceived by sin;
- Fourth, when you deceive yourself;
- Fifth, when God allows you to be deceived.

Once a person reaches the last stage of deception, the possibility of recovering and turning back to God is slim. Why? Because his voice and mercy were disregarded during the first four stages. When God allows this type of deception to proceed, it is an example of his passive wrath.

What is the wrath of God? Let us begin by seeing what it is not. God's wrath has nothing to do with him being irritable, throwing a temper tantrum, or displaying uncontrollable anger. He is the God who vindicates, but his wrath is never vindictive. God's wrath is not malicious retaliation from the hand of the All-Powerful. Rather, God's wrath is his settled hostility against sin and those who practice sin. It is a divine attribute of holiness moved into action against all unrighteousness. God's eternal displeasure is directed toward those who rebel against his authority and offend his sovereignty. The wrath of God is his justifiable indignation provoked by unsurrendered pride—it is his just, perfect, necessary, and righteous retribution against the prolonged rejection of his lordship. In essence, his wrath is his holy response to his truth being habitually denied or forsaken. His wrath is not an abstract quality, for it is part of his divine attributes just as much as love, goodness, grace, and mercy are. If God is a God of love, he is also a God of wrath.

So, what is *passive wrath*? We see it when God releases an individual from his restraining influence and therefore releases that person to live a life independent of his will. Think of Samson, who despised the conditions of his vow and chose to live outside the boundaries of God's commands. God abandoned Samson without him knowing it. One of the most terrifying verses in the Bible is, "So he awoke from his sleep, and said, 'I will go out as before, at other times, and shake myself free!' But he did not know that the LORD had departed from him" (Judges

16:20 NKJV). Think of Judas, who Christ told, at the Last Supper, to go do what's in his heart (John 13:27). God's passive wrath was upon him at that moment to carry out the desires of his own sinful passions. One of the most severe forms of judgment comes when God gives someone over to their desires and therefore allows their desires to deceive them.

Understanding The Mercy That Endures Forever

Ahab had been given opportunities to respond to God's extended compassion, but he refused to change. What happens when we exhaust God's mercy toward us? Due to the decaying of sound doctrine over the last few decades, we should ask, "Does God's mercy toward individuals ever cease?" I believe we have reached the wrong conclusions about the love and mercy of God because our premise has been wrong. A wrong beginning never leads to a right ending. Our misinterpretation of many verses concerning mercy has added to some of the confusion.

For example, the great promise in Lamentations has been severely taken out of context to support a misleading and misinformed pretext. In Lamentations 3:22–23, Jeremiah reminds us of God's awesome and great faithfulness. He also mentions that God's mercy is new each morning. This has led some to come to an incorrect interpretation of the verses. Most believe the statement means that when we get up each morning, God grants us renewed and restored mercy. Therefore, since his mercy starts over daily, it can never run out. But is this what this verse really teaches? No.

Keep in mind the book of Lamentations was written precisely because God's forbearance had run out on the people during Jeremiah's day. God declared that the people would be in captivity for 70 years, and then he would bring them back and restore them (Jer. 25:11–14; 27:21–22; 29:10–11). When Jeremiah declares that God's mercy is new every morning, he says that with each day that goes by, they are getting closer to

God's aforementioned time of deliverance. As each day goes by, they can find hope that God will return them back home, just as he had spoken.

But taking this verse out of context can greatly harm one's understanding of God's mercy. God's mercy did run out for Ahab. There is a difference between his mercy enduring forever and his mercy being extended to all continually. His mercy will endure forever because he is eternal, and his mercy is the very essence of who he was, is and always will be. Still, his Spirit will not always strive with humankind by showing us continued mercy if we don't respond to his mercy correctly.

Understanding God's Judgment

Why would God allow something he hates, like lies, to be an instrument of his judgment? When you reject God so many times and refuse to surrender to his ways, he will eventually give you over to your desires, and those desires could lead to destruction. We see this type of destruction in the Old and New Testaments. Psalm 106 reveals how the children of Israel's constant complaining caused them to forget what God had done for them, which led them to despise his counsel. They grew impatient with God's timing and began to crave or desire things outside of his will and timing, and because they refused to surrender their appetites for that which was off-limits, God gave them over to their desires, and it brought judgment to their souls (vv. 12–15). Second Thessalonians 2:9–11 says,

> The coming of the lawless one is according to the working of Satan, with all power, signs, and lying wonders, and with all unrighteous deception among those who perish, because they did not receive the love of the truth, that they might be saved. And for this reason God will send them strong

> delusion, that they should believe the lie, that they all may be condemned who did not believe the truth but had pleasure in unrighteousness. (NKJV)

God will permit delusion, so people will believe a lie. Why? This happens to people who take delight in their unrighteousness. You have to ask yourself, do you want your pleasure so badly that you will forsake God to get it? The worst thing that can happen to any believer is for God to be done with you, and you don't know it. If you are under deception, you won't know that God is done with you. To think God is with you because your life seems peaceful is self-deception.

When you become hostile toward God, you forget how God moved on your behalf. As a result, God will give you your request and allow you to decay spiritually. When this happens, what's left? We all need God's truth because we can get into a place of operating on our assumptions. Look at the rich young ruler, who thought he was approved by God because of what he had until Christ spoke. He walked away sorrowfully (Mark 9:22). This is why I love Nicodemus. He accepts the truth, even though it is offensive (John 3:10). As a result, God qualifies him to prepare Christ's body (John 19:39–40).

Some of what transpired during the COVID-19 pandemic cannot be altered. In fact, the circumstances that will follow the pandemic, whether in churches, politics, or this country as a whole, will not be "all-of-a-sudden" situations. God has already signed off on some consequences we are about to see because we held on to things we desired that were against his will. If you held onto God during the pandemic, he has surely allowed what was in your heart to surface and has given you an outlet to be healed and free. But if you did not respond to what God was doing, you may need to ask some important questions concerning where you stand with him.

Sadly, the day came when Ahab knew exactly where he stood with God. And even in his attempt to disguise himself and escape the word Micaiah spoke, God's decree still came to pass. No matter how deceptive and discreet Ahab tried to be, he could not outsmart God. Scripture tells us that a certain man drew his bow at random, striking Ahab between the joints of his armor during the battle (2 Chron. 18:33). Ahab's armor could not protect him from God's justice. God has more patience than anyone you will ever meet, but when his patience is up, no one can resist his hand (Isa. 43:13).

While Ahab appeared successful to those on earth, from heaven's perspective, he was one of the worst kings to ever rule (1 Kings 16:30). He was a king to whom God showed much mercy, yet his life ended in tragedy. Ahab was brought to Samaria and buried there, and we are left with a picture of his blood-stained chariot being washed at a pool, where dogs appeared and licked up his blood, just as God said would happen (1 Kings 22:37–38). This is not a royal way to go out, but Ahab's drawn-out rebellion toward God and his prophets cost him his life and left his troops in a vulnerable position. With no leader and defeat looming, the people had no choice but to run for their lives. This shows that when someone is rebellious, those connected to that person become the Enemy's targets (1 Kings 22:35–36).

Jehoshaphat survived a battle never intended for him, but that's because of mercy God extended (2 Chron. 18:31). He had no business joining Ahab in battle. Still, committing to what's off-limits is easy when you're deep in compromise. God gave Jehoshaphat a wake-up call when he nearly lost his life, showing it will always cost more to go against God than to follow his commands. When our compromise has grown deep, many times we need an overwhelming mercy moment that reminds us of how great God is (2 Sam. 12:13). May we learn from Jehoshaphat that God's ways might cost us relationships, popularity, and worldly success, but in the end, his way will be the only way that's still standing.

As for Zedekiah, we don't know when or how he died, but we know that Micaiah was a true prophet of the Lord, and since what he spoke about Ahab came to pass, then surely Zedekiah did not escape God's judgment either. God will not allow his true prophets to go without vindication. Zedekiah's attempt to silence and shame Micaiah with a slap would cost him in the long run (2 Chron. 18:23). In fact, we know that there would come a day when Zedekiah would go from a bold, charismatic, false spokesperson to a coward seeking safety in an inner room (18:24). It will be hard to find mercy if we've spent our days belittling God's truth and responding with deprivation when we are confronted by God's truth.

Let us remember that we are all heading toward some form of finality, and how we respond to God will determine our end.

Chapter 14

The Wake of Damage

The pandemic and the events of 2020 have seriously affected those who confess they are Christ's followers. As proof, I would bet you can look at your own church's dwindling attendance—and if not your church, then churches near you. Listen closely: you'll hear vitriol flow freely from the hearts of those who once admired the church and Christ. Examine the rise of social media accounts that specialize in convincing and coercing frustrated believers to abandon church fellowship. Look at the many recent books which ride the trending waves of today's culture. Whatever term is gaining the most buzz is being published to sell books and merchandise today. But niche marketing is not Spirit-led writing. I'm flabbergasted by the volume of Christian authors whose writings are influenced and governed by prevailing trends, not by the Spirit of God. One would have to ask themselves: how can the Holy Spirit inspire someone to write things antithetical to the scriptures? Writing to the cultural needs of the moment might get you on the best-seller list, but does it carry biblical substance for the generations that follow? A true word from God will not be trendy. It will always be timeless.

Many social media influencers increase their subscription rates and follower numbers at the expense of planting suspicion in those who are hurt, unlearned, and biblically unsound. Indeed, many influencers have already made a name for themselves by preying on people's pain, fears, insecurities, anger, injuries, and misery. What we are seeing on social media is a compelling phenomenon called *audience capture*. The clicks of an influencer's listening audience start to shape their posts, preaching, podcasts, or book writing, and therefore, they begin to mirror their audience's demands, interests, and beliefs. The audience hears what they desire, while the influencer is rewarded through monetization or by an increase in followers. Many Christian influencers have learned to appeal to their followers but have forgotten that their real audience is One. They cultivate and craft a platform and market by highlighting what their followers like. In addition, they take advantage of people struggling with real issues by misappropriating and misapplying serious terminology. Note how recently we've become familiar with the following terms once applied to vetted psychological issues but which are now freely tossed about: *toxic*, *trigger*, *abuse*, *trauma*, *narcissism*, and so on.

But the Spirit of God does not work in this manner. Anyone capitalizing on trending issues to establish a false identity, add credibility to a false narrative, or increase his or her fan base is in danger of being used by Satan. He wants to mislead people and shipwreck their faith (1 Tim. 1:19), all under the pretense of being "spiritually woke" or offering "spiritual healing." So beware of social media influencers claiming they function as apologetic and discernment ministries. While some are legitimate, others may be be used as strategic pawns of Satan to get you to question your faith, encourage you to engage in carnal living with no conviction of sin, and keep you from trusting the role of local churches.

This generation has learned to trust public figures on social media based on the number of followers they have, unaware that these individuals can hide behind the pictures and captions they post and not actively participate in a corporate fellowship that would hold them accountable. Sin enjoys like company. If I can convince you about certain things that I'm not doing, it lessens the conviction that I will have. What one posts can conceal one's pride, but spiritual testing will always reveal one's level of humility. The truth is we live in a fallen world, which means there is always an opportunity to become "triggered" in and outside the church, with believers and nonbelievers. Jesus warned that "offenses must come, but woe to the person causing the offense" (Matt. 18:7 NKJV) and that in this world, we will experience great difficulty, but then he reassured us we can be of good cheer because he has overcome (John 16:33). Believers cannot run from triggering situations for long. We will encounter them. Truth be told, a desire for God's truth will bring us into direct conflict with opposition and hardships. In fact, God is the only One who can see us through such circumstances and help us overcome situations that trouble us deeply. He does not call us to label every unpleasant issue we experience as a triggering moment or toxic; in fact, he wants us to overcome by obeying his word and not trying to control every situation by escaping. I'm not speaking of circumstances where one's life is threatened or where criminal activity is going on; I'm speaking about trials designed to be unpleasant, heart-wrenching and challenging that are necessary and sent by God to grow and to purify our hearts (1 Pet. 1:6–9; 4:12–19). Most influencers encourage believers to avoid whatever troubles them (which is oxymoronic given the advice of scriptures). They fail to offer trustworthy counsel on how to be healed because they are not healed and struggle with unresolved issues. Yet they try to convince us that they have all the answers.

The scriptures repeatedly warn about the unfruitful nature of speaking rash and idle words (Prov. 12:16–20; Matt. 12:36–37). Proverbs informs us: "A fool vents all his feelings, But a wise man holds them back" (29:11 NKJV). We've all said things from a place of hurt that we believe to be right at that moment, only to realize later that we should have kept our thoughts to ourselves. Some words you just can't get back. On the other hand, even though some may agree with our position, does heaven? This question should help us realize being led by the Spirit is paramount for every believer. When our desires and emotions are governed by God, the Spirit will produce self-control within us. This is especially true during moments of temptation when Satan is trying to capitalize on our feelings to energize us to violate the ways of God. A lack of self-control indicates that the Lord is not speaking through someone. Understand this: The first Adam missed the mark of God in the most pristine environment, but the second Adam was an overcomer in a hostile environment (Mark 1:12–13).

Once again, I am by no means gaslighting, minimizing, or trivializing away real hurt, ungodliness, and abuse. Unfortunately, these things happen—not just at church but also at our jobs and even among family members. Still, without having and seeking out biblical and mature counsel, such unresolved pain will usually draw the unhealthy attention of Satan.

It's a reality and a travesty that genuine hurt can be overlooked and mismanaged by people who use others' experiences as an opportunity to promote themselves at the expense of another's pain. In 2010 when I wrote *Shepherds, Hirelings, and Dictators: How to Recognize the Difference*, the term "spiritual abuse" was gaining momentum and attention due to unbiblical teachings and scandalous practices in the church at the time. I was contacted by an individual who had read my book and had dedicated a program on Blog Talk Radio to discuss abuses in the church. I agreed to an interview. Due to the overwhelming response to the episode, I was asked to become a weekly co-host. The weekly show had such a wide reach that national news stations would contact the show's founder whenever a scandal broke loose in the church. The weekly episodes brought in so many followers and callers that the show's owner became a national spokesperson for church-related problems.

The more people followed the program, the more disturbed I became. Not because people were escaping bad churches but because I didn't see any biblical plan being promoted to restore and repair their faith. Internally, I no longer had any peace about doing the show, so I talked with the founder. I explained my deep concerns about constantly exposing and highlighting abuse and making every show about the same old terminology usually associated with abuse but having no authentic, biblical plan to aid people's spiritual recovery. I expressed my concern that the show was turning into a sideshow to undermine the legitimate work of true pastors and the church. Because I am a pastor, I still believe in the power of the local church as an instrument for personal and spiritual growth. I believe that the believer's spiritual life must include personal connections and interaction at the local church. Christ still loves his bride and has not abandoned his intentions for the local assembly.

During the conversation, it became clear he didn't have a plan, and he didn't have the desire to devise one, for he had already achieved great publicity and success by simply talking about what was wrong with the church. So I agreed to resign from my position on the show, and needless to say, my concerns became a reality. Other guests were recruited to be the new co-hosts. They were obviously frustrated with church, and the advice they gave to all the disheartened and hurt callers was not to attend church anymore. They repeatedly said, "It's not about church—it's all about the community," "Protect your peace at any cost," "You don't need to subject yourself to a pastor—after all, he is flawed like you," and "Work on self-healing and your mental health because you don't need a pastor or a church." The rhetoric became overwhelmingly thoughtless, reckless and diabolical. Why would the Holy Spirit, through the Apostle Paul, devote three entire books known as the pastoral epistles (1 and 2 Tim. and Titus) if pastorship and a leadership structure were no longer valid? If having a pastor was not required, why would Christ give the church pastors as part of his ascension gifts (Eph. 4:7–16)? If church leadership is no longer valid, why would the Holy Spirit communicate through the writer of Hebrews about leaders "watching over the souls" of those they lead (13:17)?

The encouragement to abandon biblically ordained oversight and traditional church structures created space for people to shape Jesus into their preferred version based on their intellect, discomfort and past experiences. The overarching answer to problems had become this: "Just abandon the local church for the sake of keeping your sanity." Philosophical humanism with scripture verses sprinkled in falsely convinced many followers that they were on the road to spiritual health.

A few years later, with the growth of new social media outlets, the show had ascended to great heights, only for the owner to suddenly abandon the program altogether. The entire platform folded. This is an illustration of how the enemy of our souls works. There is always a way that seems right, but the end is destruction (Prov. 14:12). Countless hurting people had been instructed or "coached" not to trust in the church or in pastors anymore, and suddenly what fed and stoked the fire of their emotional pain was gone. People across the globe were left scattered and directionless (Matt. 9:35–36), yet they felt justified about their view of the church.

***

Throughout the years, as I've kept walking with the Lord, I've noticed that certain topics will resurface and repackage themselves in the church. You don't need prophetic discernment to know how it will all end: you just need to have a good memory. So when I see the reemergence of a term like "spiritual abuse" being parroted today, while there is validity to some cases, others have jumped on the bandwagon and use the term to appear relevant and gain credibility through capitalizing on others' victimization. For this reason, we must ensure we don't misuse or oversensitize words as clickbait or, worse, to justify spiritual rebellion.

Many people use the right terminology but with the wrong definition; therefore, they apply the word to anything they personally disagree with. The appropriate definition of spiritual abuse occurs when a position of power, influence, and oversight is used to promote self-centered desires or interests. Someone guilty of spiritual abuse is not functioning as a leader who serves but instead uses their authority to lord over others and foster and defend their own vision or needs.

Moreover, when we have experienced hurt or even read or heard stories from others of abuse, if we are not careful, that knowledge could develop a bad eye within us that questions everything from a point of view of unjust criticism or analysis. Just because a leader doesn't do things we desire them to do, or even in the manner we believe is best, that doesn't necessarily mean the leader is guilty of abuse. We will not always agree with everything that takes place within the church regarding its administration; still, not all disagreements are under the umbrella of spiritual abuse. Some issues arise simply due to personal preferences, and the judgment of right or wrong in those cases does not come down to biblical mandate.

Satan loves to travel behind the voice of God, and he will always park and rest behind a lie or spiritual hurt. He traveled behind God's voice in the garden, asking, "Did God really say?" He traveled behind the voice of God when Jesus was in the wilderness by insinuating, "If You are the Christ…," and he traveled behind God's voice in the parable of the sower (Mark 4:15). Not only is he a great deceiver, he is also great at undermining. He seeks to undermine God's truth, order, established authority, righteousness, holiness, covenant, and justice. And when he knows you have experienced frustration, disappointment, and hurt in the church, he will make sure you hear what you think you need to hear at that moment to undermine your faith and trust.

In C. S. Lewis' *The Screwtape Letters*, there is a powerful line that Screwtape, a senior-level demon, relates to Wormwood, an inferior demon, about trying to mislead believers. Screwtape tells Wormwood about the power of creating suspicion among those who follow God. He says, "Suspicion often creates what it suspects."[1] In other words, Satan specializes in bringing your private suspicions to life. This excludes sinful situations that need to be confronted: I am referring to confirming what you have suspected within yourself without God's perspective. For example, Satan is good at planting lies in your mind, and you are convinced that you are thinking correctly, not realizing what you thought was all lies. I think it's fair to say we all have been there at one point, believing how we felt and thought was correct until time revealed a different outcome. Suspicion is designed to limit your trust, where the only person you trust is yourself, and that's where Satan wants you. While God confirms his word in this hour, demons affirm planted suspicions.

***

Regarding spiritual hurt, we must keep in mind one often overlooked truth: it is not limited to congregants. In fact, pastors can experience spiritual hurt. Not every pastor is a hireling or a dictator. Some have a genuine call from Christ to lead the flock. Pastors and police officers have several things in common, and unfortunately, one thing they share is that when some are identified as corrupt or harmful, the entire group is affected. Contrary to popular opinion, there are true God-ordained pastors who don't see the church as a source of income, an enterprise, or a way to increase their social status. Some are set apart to do God's will and serve the flock.

---

[1] C. S. Lewis, *The Screwtape Letters* (New York: HarperOne, 2015), 164.

Since 2020, there have been discouraging numbers concerning the resignation of spiritual leaders. Consider the following short article:

> Barna, a Christian research organization, reported that stress, isolation and political division are some of the issues factoring into pastors' desire to quit. As of March 2022, 42% of pastors considered quitting. Why are pastors quitting?
>
> - Stress of the job
> - Loneliness and isolation
> - Political division
> - Impact on family
> - Concern about the future of the church
>
> ... Author and Pastor Glenn Packiam [spoke] about why members of the clergy are experiencing their own "great resignation." He said it became "a job that no one could actually do" as expectations increased over the years. "In the 60s or 70s, pastors were asked to become expert therapists, and to learn psychology tools, and to be able to help marriages and people with mental health issues," Packiam said. "And then somewhere in the 80s and 90s, the expectation turned towards pastors as CEOs, as entrepreneurs. And then we started adding to that."
>
> "And now they need to become social commentators, activists, experts in all of these different complex issues. And instead of these expectations being substituted to do one or another, things keep stacking [so] that things become untenable to achieve."*
>
> Social media comparisons also added to the stress of the job. During COVID, pastors felt they were being compared to other popular livestreamed church services. "You have stalking expectations, you have social media comparisons, and then you have kind of the stress fracture. The crises that we experienced in the last two years were crises that actually became the occasions for more fractures, more divisions," Packiam added.[2]

---

[2] Ashleigh Banfield, "Losing the Faith: The Great 'Pastor Resignation'," *NewsNation* (NewsNation, September 4, 2022), https://www.newsnationnow.com/banfield/losing-the-faith-the-great-pastor-resignation/. *The accompanying video contains Packiam's full statement, added here.

Some view this "great resignation" as a sign that these leaders should have never been leading in the first place. While I understand that position, I also disagree. Not every leader who has quit or is thinking about quitting is illegitimate; some are emotionally wounded and need time and space to heal.

In the scriptures, there are examples of mighty men like Elijah and Jeremiah who wanted to quit. Elijah was so discouraged that while he did not take his own life, he asked God to take it (1 Kings 19:4). I don't agree that every leader who quit was never approved by God. I see this mass resignation as Satan, once again, undermining the work of Christ in the church. We should ask ourselves, if godly leaders are quitting, then who is replacing them? Without the godly in authority, the door is wide open for wolves in shepherd's garments to enter. This leadership vacuum is an opportunity for Satan to place his self-appointed leadership to move the church off-task.

Satan is like a terrorist looking to hijack an airliner. First, he stays undercover until it's time to make himself known. Then, when he realizes he cannot accomplish his plan by remaining in coach, he looks to overtake the cockpit. If he gets control of the cockpit, all on board are under his control. Satan's goal has been to frustrate and spiritually wound leaders so much that they either transform into controlling and abusive leaders based on their unresolved personal hurt or quit so the underqualified will step up to assume their position and weaken the church.

This nation and the church are in a significant leadership crisis. To be deprived of godly leadership is worse than a famine of food and water. We see this principle in Isaiah 3. Mark this down: Anytime there is incompetent leadership, there will be a breakdown in relationships and disrespect among the people. Unfortunately, childish and incompetent leadership has taken over so much of the landscape of this country that it has cultivated an environment in which being vindictive, having no self-control, and acting brutish and entitled have become badges of self-respect. The question, "Whose side are you on?" has replaced a statement of faith for many. Unsettled hostility and juvenile anger are proposed to reflect "truth" and accepted as admirable virtues. Biblical unity—which recognizes that while personalities differ, we can all move in the same direction to achieve God's agenda—has ceased to be the benchmark of love for many. They are committed to holding on to their personal biases no matter what.

Satan's plan has been to place godly leaders in perilous situations where choices must be made. And when Satan has shaped a culture that has made the love of self the center of all things, any choice is bound to make people angry. When people become idle and only feed on what pops up on their social media feeds or on their favorite cable news station, the only opinion they will accept is the one they personally hold. When you are a leader, not everyone will always agree with your decisions. That's understandable, and leaders should be prepared to gracefully respond to those who disagree. True leadership, at times, includes the art of disappointing people whom you desire to stand firm. But when people seek to demonize a leader's character because of unpopular choices they have made, that can be unjust and pushes the envelope too far. People cross a line and lose integrity when they look to ruin, reject, and disqualify leaders who don't meet their baseless, unreasonable expectations and selfish desires. I will state this once again: this position is not meant to cover up or defend fraudulent leaders. Ungodly leaders should be held accountable. But godly leaders who display the character of Christ in word and deeds are being caught in the crossfire. They need our protection.

Vilification from those we least expect it from can be painful, perhaps especially for those of us who are leaders (Ps. 55:12–14). But a truth that's often overlooked is that we can't measure spiritual maturity by how many verses people can quote, how long they have been saved, or by how much they applaud sermons (though leaders should give people the benefit of the doubt on this last point!). As a pastor for nineteen years, I've learned through difficulties that we really don't know a person's level of spiritual maturity until they don't get their way, and that's when their hidden but true character surfaces. And we have seen over the last few years that if we disagree with someone's political party affiliation, personal preferences, and goals, they won't hesitate to criticize and abandon us. Seeing pastors and their families abruptly removed from churches and their livelihoods—not because they were sinning or teaching heretical doctrines, but simply because they didn't react in the manner the congregation considered acceptable during the presidential elections or the uproar of social disturbances—is disturbing.

I believe this contentious atmosphere has led to some godly pastors resigning from their positions. Although the hours they spend maintaining pastoral oversight are fatiguing, that factor alone likely does not account for why many leave the ministry. Some are spiritually weary because they cannot see the fruit of their labor. When national news stations or spiritual-sounding memes have more influence in a congregant's life than the countless hours of teaching and preaching that they have shouted "Amen" to, pastors are understandably pausing to reevaluate and ask themselves whether it's all worth it. Is it worth sacrificing their time, life, and family when at the end of the day, they don't have much tangible effect on the people they serve? If the people are turning to ungodly influences more than to godly leadership, the toll on pastors is high. For some, maintaining their emotional and physical health is more important than maintaining a spiritual title. Others are forcing themselves to stay in the game to avoid being seen as those who quit on God and on God's people.

However, believers, leaders, and churches do not face inevitable future doom: there is hope! What we know for certain is that Christ will continue to build his church because he said it. We know the power of death will not stop him from building his church because he said it. We know he is coming back for a glorious church without spot or wrinkle because he said it. When things start to look hopeless and discouraging, we have a true remedy: we look to him and trust what he says.

Chapter 15

Spiritual Recovery

From the pulpit to the pews, we desperately need spiritual recovery. Achieving a spiritual reset will require three ingredients: *remembering*, *repenting*, and *returning*. Removal is the only option left if these three are not accomplished. When God removes someone from his intentions, in biblical language, it's called "to perish." In Greek, it's *apollumi*. The word refers to something that has become so tainted and ruined that it is no longer suitable or usable for its intended purpose.

Because the consequences of removal are so severe, we all should pursue spiritual recovery before the window of mercy closes. May we never forget that God's mercy is never assumed by us; it's extended by his will. We don't deserve mercy; he grants it because of his lovingkindness. And when God grants you mercy, Satan will ensure that your hurts, unforgiveness, bitterness, and painful memories will cause you to miss your appointed moment of healing, victory, and restoration.

What Is the Work of Spiritual Recovery?

The working of the Spirit imparts grace to an individual, enabling them to return to a former spiritual condition. Through grace, God extends his mercy to bring restoration to someone who has experienced loss, failure, and misuse and is therefore damaged. The process of spiritual recovery is indeed painful, but it's purposeful. God is serious about his intentions. Therefore, to fully recover from damage, we must have a heart primarily concerned with his intentions and not our own interests.

Desiring to be restored just so our wishes can be accomplished will result in futile attempts at recovery (Num. 14:39–45). The process of discomfort that God has in store will always reveal any self-centered ambitions. How? Because on the road to recovery, we will find ourselves in precarious dilemmas and a season of temporary inconvenience. This is why we can't expect our environment or circumstances to be ideal. God does not mind temporarily afflicting us if he knows it will produce eternal fruit. In God's recovery plan, pain is necessary for restoration, renewal, and redemption. David understood this when he wrote, "It is good that I have been afflicted, That I may learn Your statutes." (Ps. 119:71 NKJV). The Hebrew for *afflicted* is *anah*. It does not mean being in pain due to being tormented. It means to be abased, humiliated, or humbled.

You see, the starting block of all spiritual recovery is humility. The beginning point of recovery is when we start responding to God correctly in things we embarrassingly and shamefully failed at. Failure produces that "I messed up" feeling; embarrassment concerns how people might view me when I messed up, and shame impacts how I see myself before God after failing him. God will allow us to taste shame so we don't ingest pride.

Sadly, many will miss their moment of mercy because their attachment to pride, social status, position, rank, and image will not allow them to face or endure the shame associated with being restored. There cannot be any recovery until I admit where I missed it. I am not on the road to recovery if I'm still blaming others. When Jesus was restoring Peter, after he denied Christ three times, Peter had to assume his responsibility for denying Christ in the presence of the other disciples (John 21:15–25). Why? Because his denial occurred in public, his restoration had to be in public. Trying to maintain an image and a reputation while desiring spiritual recovery is antithetical to God's ways.

In the time we live in, everything is about success, including how to constantly achieve more. There are very few books or messages on how to embrace failure. We tend to claim failure was due to being victimized. But for believers, God-induced failures are actually a pathway to unimaginable victory. When we lose, we win in many areas of our lives. One of the most beloved and quoted Psalms comes from David, who had embraced his failure. He pleaded,

> Create in me a clean heart, O God,
> And renew a steadfast spirit within me.
> Do not cast me away from Your presence,
> And do not take Your Holy Spirit from me.
>
> Restore to me the joy of Your salvation,
> And uphold me by Your generous Spirit.
> Then I will teach transgressors Your ways,
> And sinners shall be converted to You.
> (Psalm 51:10–13 NKJV)

Psalm 51 is a picture of someone who has realized that God can restore you and use your failure to teach others. Unfortunately, because of the stigma placed on failure, we tend to develop a hurt that's unhealthy for our spiritual journey. We allow personal hurt to redirect us but fail to allow the hurt of God—where we are humbled due to our failures—to direct us back to him.

God desires his hurt to be stamped on our hearts—not to keep us in perpetual guilt but to constantly remind us of who he is and what he has done. In this hour, we need spiritual leaders who can teach people to be broken over what breaks God's heart and not over what didn't work out in their own interest. God works out our failures and leads us on a path to restoration by placing us in circumstances that remind us of that failure. Of course, we want to be free from our failures without remembering them. But it has been rightly said, "If God doesn't heal us through remembering, then Satan will destroy us by remembering" (source unknown). And the first stage that must be visited in the recovery process is the emotionally painful act of remembering.

Remember

Revelation 2 begins outlining the seven types of churches that existed in times past, are operating in the present and will serve as a litmus test for churches in the future. Many interpreters believe the seven churches of Revelation 2–3 represent seven different church ages—starting with the time of the apostles and ending with the church that will be present in the end times. If that is true, then the church in Laodicea is representative of a large percentage of today's churches. Whether that interpretation is correct or not, there are overwhelming similarities between the church at Laodicea and most churches in the US.

To understand this matter in detail, we must recognize the common pattern shared by all the letters to the seven churches. Each letter is first Christ's description of himself. Second, Christ evaluates the church's condition, beginning with the phrase "I know." Third, it is the Lord's words of comfort and correction based on his irrefutable assessment of the church. Fourth, it is Jesus' command that everyone "listen to what the Spirit is saying to the churches." And fifth, it is Christ's promised blessings to those who overcome.

The first church, the church at Ephesus, had a great beginning but needed to make critical corrections if they wanted to see long-lasting fruit. This church is known as the church that lost its first love (v. 4); in reality, they never *lost* it, but rather they *left* it. It is common to hear people say that those who are most concerned with biblical doctrine and traditional Christian teaching lack true love and compassion. They point to the church at Ephesus as an example of majoring in doctrine but lacking in love for God and others. However, the church at Ephesus did not leave their first love because of doctrine but because of an internal heart issue that produced an obligatory service. The Greek for "left" in Revelation 2:4 is *aphiemi*. It means putting some distance or separation between where one is now and one's previous condition. It means to abandon, to divorce and be done with in order to go on to another thing. It's written in the aorist tense, which indicates some point in the past, but it is also in active voice, which means that the action of leaving came from the Ephesians' own volition. In other words, they chose it by their own will. These were not believers predestined to disregard their love for Christ; they chose to forsake it.

The Greek word for *first* is where we get the English word *proton*. It means first in time or rank. When a couple has a free-flowing sense of enduring love for each other during their engagement phase, but then their love becomes ritualistic over time, that is a similar picture to how the concept of leaving their first love is used in Revelation 2. Just like a married couple, we can invite God to be involved in the engagement of our journey but exclude him during the marriage of our walk. The believers of Ephesus had exchanged that which is preeminent for that which is peripheral; therefore, their service to Christ had become mechanical, taking on an obligatory tone. They neglected the spiritual passion they had for the Lord in the beginning. God frowns upon those who serve him because they feel like they have to. On the other hand, he delights in those who freely choose to serve him because they love him. Freely choosing to serve God is the foundation of biblical love. Exercising biblical love is always a choice, never a chore. It is choosing to love despite how one is treated. It is serving without receiving anything in return.

Christ does not leave this church in its weakened condition without giving them an opportunity to change their course. And as the Prophet, he gives them an ultimatum. So many times, we miss the road to recovery because Satan makes us overly sensitive to constructive criticism, and we cannot hear heavenly instructions. Sometimes God's instructions will not feel pleasant, and at times they can rattle our attitudes, but if we are drowning because of our own mistakes and a lifeline is dropped to us, we need to be open to the mercy that has been extended, and less concerned about our bruised feelings. Jesus extended a life jacket to a church that theologically knew correct teachings and how to discern between true and false apostles, but individually, the people were spiritually drowning. A breach in their hearts obstructed the flow of God's love. And his first instruction to them required them to remember where they had fallen (Rev. 2:5).

Christ asked these believers to recall or bring to mind a former moment or experience that they had in him, that not only they would know, but he would also know from first-hand interactions. The word "remember" in this verse is in the present active imperative, which means Jesus commands these believers *to be continually mindful* of their past. He calls them to take inventory of what he has done in their lives. He challenges them to remember all the memorial-stone moments they had experienced until that moment (Josh. 4:1–9). If we are going to move toward spiritual recovery, we will have to revive those "Red Sea" moments. We must call to mind those moments when circumstances looked very discouraging, but at 11:59:59, Christ showed up and gave us victory. Remembering past mercy moments should ignite hope, faith, and strength in our present moments.

A sin that many don't preach about today is the sin of forgetting. There are numerous verses in the Old Testament where God repeatedly warns the people about the dangers of forgetting (Ps. 106:13). We can forget God and his ways in times of plenty, but we can also forget the goodness of God in times of extreme adversity. The sin of forgetting is present whenever people wander away from the Lord (James 5:19–20). To reengage their love, Christ will challenge them to identify where they went wrong by examining moments between their past and present.

The Greek for *fallen* in Revelation 2:5 is in the perfect tense. It doesn't describe a fallen that is still in process but a fallen that has already reached its conclusion. Internally, the fallen ones of the church of Ephesus have reached the bottom floor of the valley, while outwardly, they still perform their duties. They are saved but in serious trouble. Christ sees through their works and sees their real issue. You may be a pastor or a spiritual leader who finds your heart does not burn with the same love and joy as it did when you first began. You may be an individual who needs to be revived from the last few years and the collateral damage that events have caused. Or you may need to be rescued from bitterness and anger. Christ is looking for you to admit you need help. He wants you to realize that if he doesn't save you, you will drown. You must come to know that he is who you need.

Repent

Admitting where we have fallen short is critical to the next stage of recovery: repentance. This stage consists of recognizing where we missed the mark and how Satan used that to further drive us away from God. It is necessary for true recovery, so much so that placing the blame on others, even God, and failing to agree with God concerning our sins will short-circuit the potency of true repentance. We might feel like we have the right to be angry at God, and that, indeed, can be a strong feeling. A strong emotional feeling, however, doesn't mean something is absolutely true. Can how we feel be cross-examined by God? Can our feelings hold up in the court of heaven, and God be found guilty? Job was sure God was his problem until God spoke (Job 40:1–8).

Holding on to unfounded feelings to maintain pride is a recipe for eternal misery. Under this demonic stronghold, one will refuse the help of God, thinking they know what's best. Don't be deceived. Satan looks to distract us in our circumstances when he sees God seeking to grant us mercy. Why? Because he was never a recipient of mercy; therefore, he works tirelessly to get us to miss our window of mercy. The mercy God offers to grant us repentance is time-sensitive; it will not always be available. Biblical repentance not only demands we acknowledge our sins but also requires that we agree with God concerning our issues. Many want to be forgiven but struggle to find agreement concerning their sins.

When Jesus began his public ministry, he preached, "Repent, for the kingdom of heaven has come near" (Matt. 4:17 NIV). Jesus was a repentance preacher! Repentance was a constant theme in all his public teachings. When he was informed that Pilate had butchered Jews from Galilee as they sacrificed at the temple in Jerusalem, Jesus preached repentance:

> Now there were some present at that time who told Jesus about the Galileans whose blood Pilate had mixed with their sacrifices. Jesus answered, "Do you think that these Galileans were worse sinners than all the other Galileans because they suffered this way? I tell you, no! But unless you repent, you too will all perish. Or those eighteen who died when the tower in Siloam fell on them—do you think they were more guilty than all the others living in Jerusalem? I tell

you, no! But unless you repent, you too will all perish."
(Luke 13:1–5 NIV)

Some people say repentance (*metanoeo* in Greek) just means to change one's mind. But it means more than that. Metanoeo suggests a radical turning away from a behavior or a sin. It is more than an intellectual idea. It stresses a person's turning around in totality. It's a complete alteration of one's life which requires abandoning an old way and being willing to embrace a new direction.

Judas, for example, had a change of mind brought on by remorse, but he did not have a change of heart. A change of heart is accompanied by repentance.

> When Judas, who had betrayed him, saw that Jesus was condemned, he was seized with remorse and returned the thirty pieces of silver to the chief priests and the elders. "I have sinned," he said, "for I have betrayed innocent blood." (Matt. 27:3–4)

True repentance would have turned Judas from his sin to plead to God for mercy. Instead, he looked for an opportunity to alleviate his guilt, which in his case, led to suicide. "So Judas threw the money into the temple and left. Then he went away and hanged himself" (Matt. 27:5). Repentance involves sorrow for the act of sin, while remorse involves only sorrow for its consequences (2 Cor. 7:8–12). A repentant person is sorry they sinned, whereas a remorseful person is sorry they got caught. A repentant person shares in carrying the hurt of Christ; a remorseful person carries personal shame, which is not a guarantee for real change.

Louis Berkhof describes biblical repentance as a change of view, a change of feeling, and a change of purpose. He writes that it is "a change of view, a recognition of sin as involving personal guilt, defilement, and helplessness; a change of feeling, manifesting itself in sorrow for sin committed against a holy God; a change of purpose, an inward turning away from sin, and a disposition to seek pardon and cleansing."[1]

This view of penitence is severely absent in the life of many believers today. Simply asking God to forgive us is less offensive to seeker-friendly audiences than recognizing our dire situation of guilt and defilement and our need for pardon and cleansing. If asking for forgiveness does not yield eternal fruit, such a request is hollow.

The message Jesus preached is the same message we desperately need today: repentance. Repentance is not simply about changing our minds; it is a turning from our sin, compromise, and delusional views. Repentance will always be on the heart of God when his people are drifting away. When the church is falling in love with the world and becoming adulterers and enemies of God (James 4:4), God's heart does not call for us to be more relevant, dream big visions, maximize our investments, or pursue our goals. Instead, it calls for us to return to our first love. The believers in Ephesus are called to remember and repent with no delay. When the Spirit of God compels us to repent, Satan will ensure we are distracted and full of excuses. So, on the day we hear God's voice, let us not harden our hearts.

Return

The last step in spiritual recovery is returning—doing the deeds we once did. Notice how "doing the deeds" has nothing to do with adding more activities to our plate but has everything to do with returning to Christ. It consists of returning to a time when our motivations were untainted—again, it's similar to the love a man and a woman have for one another during their engagement season. When we return to our first love, hidden issues of the heart no longer hinder that love. It's when they are hidden that we feel obligated and act out of rote, ritual

---

[1] Louis Berkhof, *Systematic Theology* (Grand Rapids: Eerdmans, 1939), 492.

duty. The practices of remembering and repenting have reached down into the unknown chambers of the heart and found some evil there (Ps. 139:23–24), and once we have been set free from such evil, a new and vibrant love for Christ himself springs forth.

This is the type of remembering, repenting, and returning Christ desires once again for all who have become spiritually disjointed and lack the peace and joy they once walked in. I believe many will have a short window to receive this offer from Christ. But what if some refuse to respond? What are the consequences of rejecting his mercy? God's judgment. This has always been God's way, from the times of Noah to the church in Ephesus, in the book of Revelation, and even in our days. When nations and people trample God's mercy underfoot, God does not hide his displeasure; he makes them an open example of his rejection so that others can repent and turn to him.

Jesus tells the believers in Ephesus that their first love can be restored, but they have to do it his way, on his terms, and in his timing. He warns, "Remember therefore from where you have fallen; repent and do the first works, or else I will come to you quickly and remove your lampstand from its place—unless you repent" (Rev. 2:5 NKJV). There are no other options or excuses. "Or else" speaks of a terrifying outcome: if they do not remember and repent, he will come to them and remove their lampstand. When Christ uses the phrase "I will come," he is not speaking about his second coming. He is speaking about his judgment coming at any moment if we refuse to hear his voice. And the result of his judgment is that he will remove the light we initially had.

***

God is serious about his mercy being heard and obeyed. I pray this chapter has helped uncover things that cause you to see God, circumstances, and your actions from a new perspective. I hope that, like Jehoshaphat, you will go back and remember God's goodness and faithfulness throughout the years and return to the God whose character is beyond reproach and whose heart you will never find in any other person. May remembering his past mercies transform and encourage you in the present season and stimulate your hope for the future.

Chapter 16

The Way Forward

As I mentioned in Chapter 1, my intention in writing *Hostility Within* was to accomplish three distinct goals and to highlight eight characters and their individual traits that we have seen emerge in the church during and in the post-pandemic era. To conclude our study, let's review them. As we examine and apply the lessons from scripture to the culture around us, I believe God will show us the way forward in our lives individually and for the church as a whole.

Be Equipped to Handle Spiritual Adversity

My first goal has been to help equip the body of Christ for a time of intense diabolical activities that I believe many in the church are not adequately equipped to handle. Over the years, a lack of sound biblical teaching has left many ignorant of and vulnerable to satanic schemes. Therefore, many have found themselves spiritually sinking and failing to successfully navigate this extremely difficult time. I believe the first step in helping people walk circumspectly in emotionally painful seasons is to announce what to expect and how to respond. Jesus never shielded his followers from what they should expect, and he never failed to give them his expectation for how they should respond (John 15:18–21; 16:33).

In our attempt to "win the world at any cost," we have paid a hefty price. We have attempted to be more loving, relevant, and appealing to seekers, which has left many as spiritual infants unable to maneuver through issues that require spiritual maturity. But maturity cannot be achieved when we only teach the good or "positive" things from the Bible while ignoring what we perceive to be unpopular, uncomfortable, irrelevant, and "negative." In the days of Ezekiel the prophet, God commanded him to eat the scroll (Ezek. 2:9–10; 3:1–3). Scrolls at the time had writing on one side only. However, the scroll that God charged Ezekiel to eat had writing on both sides (2:10). The double-sided scroll is significant: it limited the prophet from trying to modify God's message to accommodate his own personal wishes. Because a double-sided scroll was so uncommon then, when God showed one to Ezekiel it implied that the message was complete. God didn't need any input from the prophet's own will to manufacture a message. In essence, Ezekiel was commanded to eat the whole scroll like we are instructed to preach, teach, and live—by God's whole counsel.

However, because of the increased presence and pressure of those who seek their own desires, some churches have limited teaching to subjects that are not controversial, convicting, or negative. They know people shrink, run, blame others or rebel when challenged by teachings that make them uncomfortable, and the church wants to keep as many people as possible in attendance. However, when God's full counsel is rejected, true biblical discipleship suffers. By teaching people to draw some direction from scripture but not expecting full discipleship from them, the church has been left in a fractured state.

What should we be prepared for in the days to come? Diabolical hatred, destructive divisiveness, disheartening betrayal, demoralizing offenses, disengaging lies, damaging relationships, deception and distrust are coming (if they're not already here). Can such things be prevented? No. Perhaps that surprises you. But if we are determined to follow God's prescribed way and will, we will face these challenges. In the eight signs mentioned in Matthew 24, Jesus said these things must happen (see Chapter 3, "A Precursor Season: The Signs Emerge"). They are painful, undesirable, and sometimes seem unfair, but they are already determined. Therefore, it is incumbent on us to learn how to discern when these times are upon us. Then we can learn how to walk in a way that will please our Lord—with righteousness, integrity, holiness, and love. On the other hand, if we are not properly equipped, we have the potential to shape the church in such a way that carnal and irrational behavior will lead unbelievers to question its sacredness, and it could become a place where the name of Christ is misaligned and blasphemed. This is the end goal of our Adversary.

Leave Behind a Victim Mentality and Look to God

My second goal was to help those who have become victims of unexplained and unanswered adversity. Adverse circumstances can cause us to question God's love. In these moments, Satan looks to hijack the believer's wavering faith due to their unquenchable pain. He takes great delight in fishing in the hearts of the discouraged and disturbed. He takes great pride in convincing Christ followers that their Commander has failed and forsaken them. When believers become more visually oriented rather than focusing on being hearers of the word of God, we become extremely vulnerable to attacks designed to offend us. When believers become offended, they subsequently become confused. It is dangerous for sheep in a discouraging situation to be angry with their Shepherd.

If I am in a confused state of mind or season, Satan looks to have me devalue my spiritual privilege as a son or daughter of Christ by overemphasizing my discomfort or what I dislike. His motive is to restructure my theological perspective. We see this happening in Asaph's life in Psalm 73. Who was Asaph? He wrote twelve of the Psalms—his name is in their superscriptions. King David chose him as a prophet to lead worship and minister over the Ark of God (1 Chron. 16:1–6). Why would a person of this caliber care about the wicked prospering (Ps. 73:3)? Why would he question if he had cleaned his heart in vain (v. 13)? How could a man chosen to worship before the Ark think about turning his back on God (vv. 2,15)?

When areas in our hearts are not in full compliance with God's will, and Satan is pressing us, he will highlight our personal discontent and get us to overlook our spiritual privilege. If we give in to a disgruntled mindset, we grant him access to accomplish his objective. Make no mistake about this one truth: Satan has an objective, and it's not always obvious. Because God deals in objectives, Satan has an objective. To execute his plan, he mimics God's kingdom. In Asaph's case, the real issues were not that the wicked prosper or other discouraging things he saw. Those things were the bait; they were the offense-makers. They were only issues to Asaph because something in his heart made them an issue. Asaph's personal issues became a spiritual distraction, and we are subject to the same weakness. Satan looks for this type of distraction to execute his plan against us. His purpose is to convince us that the God we serve and give up our lives for is no longer trustworthy. It's hard to fully trust in a God we feel is not fair, and it's hard to lay down our lives for God when we are suspicious of his dealings toward us. Satan knows once he can convince us that God is not fair or good, then he can get us to devalue a spiritual privilege that we didn't deserve but have received.

That leads to Satan's ultimate objective: to get us to betray God and those who once respected our spiritual opportunities that we now could care less about.

In the days to come, we must be careful not to allow offenses to dominate our hearts or cause us to question God's love. God's love is not always manifested through things he has the right and power to stop or grant. On many occasions, his love manifests itself in how he has prepared us for those things. When he has prepared us for something, we will endure it joyfully because of his love. We need to avoid limiting our understanding of his love to what he prevents or permits. We don't want to be guilty of overlooking love that comes in the form of warnings and restrictions.

While attempting to pull up those believers who have become victims, I have also desired to reach those kidnapped by deep hurt, bitterness and anger, which has caused them to turn their back on Christ and his church—those who used to enjoy and look forward to going to God's house, who now believe that a local fellowship is no longer necessary. Allow me to speak directly:

You never believed this until you got hurt. Over time, your heart has grown cold and callous. Your former testimony was that you could not wait until church began. For many, you were the Uber driver before there was such a company. You joyfully transported those who had no transportation to church. You delighted in being a vessel God could trust to bring people to church. The time is up for you to justify why you are not seeking God because you are hurt or angry. People indeed get hurt by others in the church, and though it doesn't make it right, it shouldn't hinder what you owe Christ for redeeming you. And you're not alone: for David, Jeremiah, Jesus, and Paul, their most painful injuries did not come from people of the "world"—they came from people who said they knew God. But they did not allow hurt to hinder their seeking of God.

Let me note once again that I'm not speaking about cases where a crime was committed against someone or where someone was assaulted, demeaned, or otherwise seriously violated. I'm referring to personal disagreements or offenses that happen in church, at work or even at home that cause us to feel angry or disturbed. Sometimes God allows us to be hurt in a church because we were in the wrong location. And because God's will is determined by specific locations, he may move us by his providence through the hurt. Sometimes we take the pain personally, and it damages us. But God desires that the pain redirects us to his will.

Isolating ourselves from true believers is not the answer. It only leads to increased spiritual callousness. Solomon writes, "A man who isolates himself seeks his own desires; He rages against all sound wisdom" (Prov. 18:1). The longer we withdraw from other believers, the more we will start to live a life that's focused only on the self. Solomon also notes, "The backslider in heart will be filled with his own ways, But a good man will be satisfied from above" (Prov. 14:14). Self-centered living is the default position when we forsake God. Something has to fill the void that God once occupied, and self will unashamedly answer that call. With a self-centered mindset, not only will one start to love self over God and others, but one will also start to despise sound wisdom. Solomon also said such people will "rage against counsel." Counsel that doesn't support their desires will be met with destructive anger and contempt.

If you recognize these tendencies in yourself, be aware that you are in a bad place.

The only remedy is repenting and asking the Lord to free you from bitterness. Don't be a causality of this battle. God is willing to heal you if you are willing to turn from yourself. There is a difference between being broken and wounded. Brokenness is an earmark of the believer's life. It is the mark of a humble, obedient, and contrite heart (Ps. 51:17). A person with a wounded spirit has suffered such hurt or disappointment that their will and emotions refuse to be comforted. Therefore, they fester and brood resentment internally. Anger will reveal itself externally in explosive responses, extreme mood swings, blaming others, and an uncontrollable attitude. A person who is wounded focuses so much on their injuries that they live within their wounds, which causes their mindset to become so negative that hearing God's instructions becomes challenging. Think of the oldest son in the parable in Luke 16. He was so dissatisfied with his father's decisions that the father's viewpoint could not reroute his anger (v. 28). God may not always do things we think are acceptable, but he will always act based on his goodness. David says it well in Psalm 147: "He heals the brokenhearted and binds up their wounds" (v. 3). Seeking the Lord while he may be found is the true medicine for a bitter soul (Heb. 12:12–17).

True Leaders Can Regain the Faith and Strength to Answer the Call

My third goal was to help wounded and overwhelmed spiritual leaders. Biblical, inspired leaders are essential to the heart of Christ. They are so dear to him that he gave leaders as his gift to the church (Eph. 4:7–16). Being trusted to oversee a flock of people is a daunting and, at times, undesirable task. Yet, it's also rewarding. To be chosen by the Chief Shepherd as one of his under-shepherds is one of the greatest responsibilities a person can have on this side of heaven. The number of pastors burning out is alarming. Without true shepherds occupying leadership roles, it's easier for Satan to raise up counterfeit spokespersons to assume those positions. Part of Satan's end-time plan is to weary and disarm biblically-qualified spiritual leaders. As they leave their original posts, the unqualified in Christ's church take over and lead the church to destructive ends.

Consider an incident concerning the wicked King Jeroboam. Because of his wickedness, many true priests left the northern kingdom and traveled to strengthen the hands of Solomon's son, Rehoboam (2 Chron. 11:13–17). Their departure opened the door for Jeroboam to consecrate whomever he desired as priest (1 Kings 13:33–34). Only those from the tribe of Levi were to be appointed as priests, but Jeroboam didn't think much of obeying God's commands. Subsequently, his rebellion and unauthorized leadership eventually led the people into sin (2 Kings 17:21–23). This was Satan's plan then, and it is his plan today.

A Personal Note to Former and Weary Leaders:

Therefore, I admonish God's leaders who left overseeing the flock of God for roles such as "spiritual advisor" or "church consultant" to get back into the everyday business of the work of the ministry. We need your boots on the ground, not your feet propped up. Come off the golf course and get back into the battle. The people recognized Joshua's potential for leadership, but Moses stayed visible until God took him home. Elijah became weary, but God strengthened him to finish his assignment. May you hear the voice of the Spirit and be revived and recharged to return to your duty.

I also admonish the leaders who have stayed in position but find their attitude toward ministry has become purely obligatory and no longer lead with joy. You may never get the respect and appreciation you believe you have earned from those you lead, so shift your focus to the One who sees everything. Several years ago, while preaching in a different state, a heavy cloud of discouragement suddenly engulfed me. I felt unappreciated at the church where I was ministering. In the midst of that heaviness, I heard a small but firm voice in my heart. The question, "Is heaven not enough?" rang loudly within my spirit. My demeanor immediately shifted, and the discouragement vanished. God was adjusting my attention from things of this world to see things from his perspective. Great joy flooded my heart, knowing I serve a Lord who sees and is a very present help.

May the joy of the Lord be your strength and hope. May the words of the elder Peter cause you to catch your second wind:

> And now, a word to you who are elders in the churches. I, too, am an elder and a witness to the sufferings of Christ. And I, too, will share in his glory when he is revealed to the whole world. As a fellow elder, I appeal to you: Care for the flock that God has entrusted to you. Watch over it willingly, not grudgingly—not for what you will get out of it, but because you are eager to serve God. Don't lord it over the people assigned to your care, but lead them by your own good example. And when the Great Shepherd appears, you will receive a crown of never-ending glory and honor. (1 Pet. 5:1–4 NLT)

Final Reflections on the Characters and Lessons of 2 Chronicles 18

Throughout *Hostility Within*, we've studied the characters from Second Chronicles 18: God, the lying spirit, the people, Micaiah, Zedekiah, the false prophets, Jehoshaphat, and Ahab. These eight reflect personality traits currently operating in the body of Christ both during and post-pandemic. Learning to identify their traits and how they appear in those around us is essential to being able to recognize the traits in our own lives. We can fail to notice problems in our hearts until God allows challenging circumstances and people to reveal what's in us.

Let's review the characters and their traits.

God

Second Chronicles 18 allows us to see from God's perspective and reveals some of his attributes normally hidden from human sight.

> **Sovereignty**—God is in control of all circumstances, even when things seem chaotic or out of control.
>
> **Mercy**—When that which is deserved is withheld to the benefit of the recipient, mercy is in action. It's compassion toward someone that one has power over to harm or afflict. When God overrides what is lawful and right and extends forbearance, that is mercy. It's the kindness shown to one who offends the heart of God.
>
> **Long-suffering**—God can show patience with those who don't deserve it. He can endure long trials with people and is slow to anger.
>
> **Wrath**—God's wrath reflects his justifiable indignation, which is provoked by unsurrendered pride. It's his settled hostility against sinful practices and people who are unresponsive to his patience. It's his eternal displeasure directed at those who offend his goodness and rebel against his authority.

We learn that unpleasant things happening on earth could directly correlate with what God has purposed in heaven. Not seeing circumstances from God's perspective can cause us to respond in ways that contradict God's will.

Things to Remember:

In times of crisis and conflict, many things are important but not essential. Two essentials are God's perspective and his timing. Without seeking these two things, we make decisions that can have negative long-term consequences. When God grants mercy, it's not so one can stay in sin but so one can turn to God and live.

~*~

The Lying Spirit

This evil spirit is not spoken about by many today. This is unfortunate, considering this spirit is sweeping throughout the US and the church. In Chapter 7, "The Lying Spirit," we saw how this spirit works and how successful it is. Who the Holy Spirit is to God, this spirit is to Satan. Where there is deception, a lying spirit is present. Deception consists of using a lie to promote something that is not of value. Therefore, the intent of deception is to exchange something of inferior value for something of greater value. Why are lies believable? Because they appeal to the flesh. They confirm and strengthen something in humanity's fallen nature. They create a sense of security and confidence. They allow individuals to live in an illusion to escape the realities of the present. They fortify a person's self-worth and importance. But in spite of the self-gratifying promises of these things, at the end of it all, it is a lie. Because a lie is so unsure of its rhetoric, it never looks to stand alone. To make it seem credible, it recruits others to repeat its language mindlessly. These indicate a lying spirit is present: false prophets, false witnesses, and conspiracy theorists. They will twist scripture, promote unhealthy compromise, give misinformation, spout propaganda, overlook hypocrisy, and influence spiritual apostasy. The only answer to overcoming lies is to pursue and live out God's truth.

Things to Remember:

Truth loves to convey, while lies exist to convince. A lie is determined and passionate in its pursuit and has nothing to lose. Why? Because it had nothing to lose in the beginning.

~*~

The People

Lies muddy the water, so in their presence, the people, as bystanders, are unsure of what to believe. We saw in our story that God was merciful in warning the people. But they were caught in a dilemma because they heard stances on polar opposites. This is part of Satan's plot to cause people to make consequential choices. We see a similar situation when Elijah addresses the people about who they are going to serve, and the people answer not a word (1 Kings 18:21). We see it when the false prophet Hananiah confronts Jeremiah in the presence of the people, with a "Thus says the Lord" word that contradicts Jeremiah's previous prophecy (Jer. 28:1–17).

In our story, God, in his love, was informing the people ahead of time of the danger of making the wrong decision (2 Chron. 18:16, 27), but as usual, people tend to trust the lie over trusting what's true. We don't know how much we value a thing until God speaks concerning that particular thing.

Things to remember:

At the beginning, there are three answers to every question: God's, Satan's, and man's opinions. In the conclusion, there will be only two possibilities: God's and Satan's. Man's opinion will either confirm God's rule or merge with Satan's lie. The majority's opinion doesn't mean it's the right opinion. Walking in the counsel of the ungodly will not yield the peaceable fruit of righteousness (Ps. 1:1). Learning to discern between contradictory statements will be paramount in the coming days.

~*~

Micaiah

Micaiah was the true spokesperson for the Lord. We learned two things in particular. First, in an avalanche of deception, the truth will always be outnumbered by lies. But truth doesn't need to be believable for it to be true. Truth doesn't need props or dramatic displays of showmanship to appear credible: it can stand on its own. Second, if we speak the truth in a post-truth culture, we will face opposition and vitriol. King Ahab's exact words about Micaiah were, "I hate him." It's one thing for the world to despise us: Jesus said they would (John 15:18–20). It's another thing when anger, resentment, and retaliation come from people who claim to call on God's name.

What prompted Ahab to feel such hatred for God's prophet? Here are Ahab's exact words: "I hate him because he never prophesies good concerning me, but always evil." A love-of-self philosophy has planted itself right in the house of God, and anything spoken that is unfavorable to the people's desires will get the speaker on the people's *Most Wanted* list. God did not send Micaiah to change the king's heart but to show his mercy to the people. Micaiah's presence also revealed God's perspective on what was happening. Without a true word from God, we are left to perceive things in the natural by what we see in the natural.

Things to remember:

Lies run fast while the truth walks slow. In a famous quotation commonly attributed to Mark Twain, "A lie can travel halfway around the world before truth puts on its shoes." The irony of this statement is that it was made before the invention of social media. Truth-tellers in these Last Days will have to learn how to overcome rejection, function through criticism, stand firm in the midst of insults, and endure mockery. Speaking the truth is never popular, but it's necessary.

~*~

Zedekiah

Zedekiah was the leading spokesperson for the lie. We've seen characters like Zedekiah run rampant throughout the body of Christ both during and in the post-pandemic eras. These actors use character assassination as an underhanded tactic because they are deficient in the truth, and therefore, they lack integrity in their arguments. A Zedekiah-like character is skilled in presentation and persuasive in arguments, but the source of their competency is a lying spirit (2 Chron. 18:10). This character lives for the attention of the crowd. When the applause around someone is greater than the substance in them, the crowd will eventually ruin them. The lie's spokesperson generally has a brash attitude that speaks with confidence and assurance but is clueless about their true spiritual condition. Zedekiah proclaimed, "Thus says the Lord," unaware an evil spirit was speaking through him. Becoming one with a lying spirit can empower someone to feel emboldened and behave in such a way that they fully persuade themselves that what they say and do is from God, and they do not realize they are working on Satan's behalf. Zedekiah was so convinced by his own self-deception that he slapped God's servant without any fear of God (v. 23).

Things to Remember:

Anything Satan uses will eventually come to a bad ending. Not allowing God to get to the hidden issues of the heart invites Satan to borrow one's tongue, which is designed to lead others astray. Solomon writes, "He who hates, disguises it with his lips, And lays up deceit within himself" (Prov. 26:24 NKJV). Someone with this character trait may seem like they have gotten away with such treasonous acts because sometimes the justice of God tarries. Still, it never sleeps forever, for the scriptures warn us that he who speaks lies will not escape (Prov. 19:5). We know when that day came that this man, bold and pretentious in public, was reduced to a coward hiding (2 Chron. 18:24).

~*~

The False Prophets

Individuals sent by Satan to misrepresent God's character and agenda are false prophets. Since the days of Moses, God has been candid about their emergence. Why? Because they are raised up and sent by Satan (Jer. 14:14) to malign God's image and move God's people onto ungodly paths. False prophets will always have a market for two reasons: first, they specialize in saying what people have an appetite to hear, and second, Satan induces them to proclaim words of confirmation to those with idols in their hearts (Ezek. 14:1–11). Satan's agenda in sending untruthful prophets into the house of God is to get God's people to believe in a false promise or future so that in the end, when the promise doesn't come to pass, people will form an unfavorable opinion concerning God's character. Satan will use this wrong conclusion to distort and dismantle peoples' perception of God's faithfulness and reliability. Who would lay down their lives for an untrustworthy God? This is the end goal of Satan through all false prophets.

Things to Remember:

False prophets are not just dangerous because of what they say: what makes them lethal is who they claim they represent. If you cannot determine who is true and who is false, it's an indicator that you cannot distinguish God from Satan. In our story in 2 Chronicles, the false prophets used God's name to give their damaging words credibility (2 Chron. 18:5,9,11,21–22).

The ratio was 400 false prophets against one true prophet. There will always be more of what's false than what is real. When you see a surplus of those who call themselves prophets, beware that Satan may be present, and God may be bringing judgment to a situation. Remember that when a lying spirit is in the land, prophetic "confirmation" does not automatically indicate the message is from God. Ahab had 400 confirmations, but not one was from the Lord.

~*~

Jehoshaphat

He was a true man of God initially, but through compromise, Jehoshaphat was influenced by the lie. Yet he still found mercy from God. We learned that no matter how great one starts their journey with God, compromise can ruin its fruitfulness. Truth is eroded where compromise is accepted. Everything went King Jehoshaphat's way until his loyalty to Ahab placed him in a dangerous battle that almost cost his life (2 Chron. 18:31). God was so angry with Jehoshaphat's choice to follow Ahab's lies that God had to reveal to him how close he was to death (2 Chron. 19:1–3). Jehoshaphat shows us that compromise is deadly to a believer's walk. It weakens godly principles and standards and reduces the quality and value of one's convictions, resulting in conformity to a substandard measurement.

Things to Remember:

Blind loyalty is no loyalty at all. When one is devoted to something rooted in deception, loyalty can become lethal. Without Jehoshaphat's rejection of the 400 prophets' prophecies, God's true prophet would have remained in obscurity. Jehoshaphat was not driven by confirmations; he wanted to know the truth. In the days to come, we can't be so driven toward things that affirm our desires that they hinder our search for God's truth. Many times God's truth will not agree with our desires, plans, or goals, but his way will always be good and perfect. In Jehoshaphat's mistakes, we see the mercy of God. Until you conclude that nothing about you is deserving, it's impossible to fully embrace such undeserved mercy.

May those who have made bad decisions since the pandemic find the strength to cry out for God's mercy. He is willing if we are determined.

~*~

Ahab

Ahab was the king controlled by a lie. He mistreated God's messenger and therefore experienced the wrath of God. Addicted to immoral activities, his heart brazened against any righteous work. His appetite for perversion and distorted belief system created hostility against God and truth. Ahab was idolatrous, self-governed and believed God existed to sign off on his wishes. He viewed God's will as optional. His personal wishes were his priority. Sadly, despite God's extended patience, Ahab's hostility within was too much to overcome, and he came to a shameful, painful end.

Things to Remember:

Two diametrically opposed belief systems operate within the church—humanism and theocentrism.

Humanism *is a system of thoughts centered on us and our own pleasure. It looks to substitute and supplant God's truth, reality and requirements into something that caters to personal preferences. Humanism places our needs, desires, comfort and wills at the center of God's plan. Therefore, the end of all things is one's happiness.*

A theocentric mindset *reflects when one lives and makes adjustments in a way that puts God at the center, making him the main focus. This mindset realizes that everything flows from God and is generated by him. The end of all things is to glorify God.*

In these post-pandemic days, a great acceleration in the desire to love the self has occurred (2 Tim. 3:1–2). But if we desire God to be the author of our lives, we will have to be willing to be misunderstood and misdiagnosed. We will have to overcome rejection and resist the wave of end-time apostasy destined to strike the church. Unfortunately, many who have tasted the goodness of God and witnessed his power will be swept away as they adopt mindsets like Ahab's and undermine the moments of mercy God has given to turn their hearts back to him.

~*~

Final Prayer and Reminder

I pray that this book has accomplished its goal. I pray that we as a church have learned and gained a different perspective from reading this book concerning the pandemic. I hope we learn from hindsight— it can give us great insights concerning our present so we can readjust our spiritual lens for the future. The coming days will be challenging for the church, but I pray that by being set free from the hostility within, we avoid the traps of the enemy. I pray that the church will shake off her wounds from 2020 and rise up and be that city set on a hill, that lighthouse that shines brightly in the midst of calamity, the salt that doesn't lose its flavor.

Despite whatever challenges you may need to overcome to be healed from a discouraged and angry heart, always remember this: As we can walk through a puddle, so our God can walk through any Red Sea.

About the Author

~*~

Tavares D. Robinson is the founder and senior pastor of Sound the Trumpet Ministries of Miami, located in Miami, Florida, where he has served for nineteen years. He also serves as the founder of Watchman Publishing and The Watchman Podcast. The Lord has graced Robinson with a bold prophetic voice that turns people's hearts back to God. He is the author of four previous books: *Shepherds, Hirelings and Dictators: How to Recognize the Difference* (now in its second edition), *The Utopia of a Strange Love: When the Love of God is Mishandled*, *Warnings from the Garden: Uncovering the Wiles of Deception*, and *The Process of Transition: Reforming the Heart for Growth*. While each of Robinson's books has its own specific focus, each provides believers with the necessary tools to identify truth and to discern authentic from spiritually unhealthy leadership. Robinson currently lives with his family in South Florida.

~*~

More From
Tavares D. Robinson

Throughout the generations, false prophets and insincere teachers have pretended to have the best interests of God's people in mind. They claim they are human instruments who have received direct words of the Lord through the Holy Spirit. But in the final analysis, they do not represent God, and they harm the sheep often to the point of costing them their souls.

Who are these deceitful shepherds and how can we distinguish a true shepherd from wolves in shepherd's clothing? That is the question Pastor Tavares Robinson explores in *Shepherds, Hirelings and Dictators: How to Recognize the Difference*. In this new tenth-anniversary edition, Pastor Robinson takes the reader on a biblical journey as he addresses many of today's toughest issues surrounding dishonest shepherds.

"If you want to be cured you will not argue about the taste of the medicine…Deception is rampant in the church. We must confront it boldly, without fear, and Shepherds, Hirelings and Dictators helps us do just that. Pastor Robinson does not waste or mince his words and he makes no apologies for telling the truth that needs to be heard in these days of apostasy. This book is an excellent and much needed source written by a godly pastor who loves the body of Christ and yet sees a massive apostasy and departure from the pure gospel of Jesus Christ."

TavaresRobinson.org
Available at most major online book retailers

MORE FROM
TAVARES D. ROBINSON

In *The Process of Transition: Reforming the Heart for Growth*, Pastor Robinson details the process of the believer's life as a necessary step for growth. He recalls a statement from a neighbor who is a pilot: "For us as pilots, it's all about the journey, but for passengers, it's all about the destination." Believers are often impatient and desire results immediately. But Robinson explains the four steps to becoming transformed by God's work in our lives: detachment, disidentification, disappointment and disconcertment. What do these four steps lead to? Transformation. But when? This book highlights God's promise to those who persevere.

"A tell-all that shines light on the real path to truly becoming transformed in God."

TAVARESROBINSON.ORG
Available at most major online book retailers

MORE FROM
TAVARES D. ROBINSON

They are ubiquitous these days—eloquent, charismatic preachers, speakers, teachers, and evangelists who skillfully argue that the essential message of Christianity is love. But there are other fundamentals of being a follower of Christ that the popular preachers often ignore. The lack of teaching on it is not just misleading but dangerous. In *The Utopia of a Strange Love: When the Love of God is Mishandled*, Pastor Robinson identifies, explores, and discusses the problem, and then challenges readers to get back to the basics in order to recover the true historical meaning of God's love.

"…will take you back to a biblical love of God that is discerning, dividing truth from the lie, where the love of God pushes you out of the realms of comfortable man-made concepts…"

TAVARESROBINSON.ORG
Available at most major online book retailers

MORE FROM
TAVARES D. ROBINSON

The problem of deception and bowing to the culture goes all the way back to the Garden of Eden, where Adam and Eve became the Serpent's first victims. They began to see circumstances, themselves, and life in general from Satan's point of view, and God's authority was no longer the centerpiece of their lives. *Warnings from the Garden: Uncovering the Wiles of Deception* addresses the many landmines our Adversary has planted among us. It will also help readers uncover errors and recover a passion for historical biblical truths, producing a true conformity to Christ.

"A must-read if you yearn for a bold voice on this topic in the midst of theologically censored, commercialized, seeker-friendly fluff."

TAVARESROBINSON.ORG
Available at most major online book retailers

The Watchman Podcast is a scripture-based podcast that seeks to warn with sound principles and safeguard God's church with His truth. Join us as we explore biblical topics and discover what God's Word has revealed regarding spiritual matters.

~*Find it on major podcast platforms*~

www.ingramcontent.com/pod-product-compliance
Lightning Source LLC
Chambersburg PA
CBHW060353080526
44583CB00012B/290